NOLO'S LAW FORM KIT

Wills

By Attorney Denis Clifford & Lisa Goldoftas

NOLO PRESS BERKELEY

YOUR RESPONSIBILITY WHEN USING A SELF-HELP LAW KIT

We've done our best to give you useful and accurate information in this kit. But this kit does not take the place of a lawyer licensed to practice law in your state. If you want legal advice, see a lawyer. If you use any information contained in this kit, it's your personal responsibility to make sure that the facts and general information contained in it are applicable to your situation.

KEEPING UP-TO-DATE

To keep its kits up-to-date, Nolo Press issues new printings and new editions periodically. New printings reflect minor legal changes and technical corrections. New editions contain major legal changes, major text additions or major reorganizations. To find out if a later printing or edition of any Nolo kit is available, call Nolo Press at (510) 549-1976 or check the catalog in the *Nolo News,* our quarterly newspaper.

To stay current, follow the "Update" service in the *Nolo News.* You can get a two-year subscription by sending us the registration card in this kit. In another effort to help you use Nolo's latest materials, we offer a 25% discount off the purchase of any new Nolo kit or book if you turn in any earlier printing or edition. (See the "Recycle Offer" in the back of this booklet.)

FIRST EDITION	
Third Printing	February 1998
BOOK DESIGN	Terri Hearsh
COVER DESIGN	Brad Thomas
PRODUCTION	Stephanie Harolde
PRINTING	Consolidated Printing

ISBN 0-87337-181-X

TABLE OF CONTENTS

HOW TO USE THIS KIT

This kit contains fill-in-the-blank will forms that are valid in the District of Columbia and every state but Louisiana.[1] Following the step-by-step instructions in this kit, you can create your own will that:

- leaves your property to people and organizations of your choice

- names someone to care for your minor children and manage their property, and

- names someone to make sure the terms of your will are carried out.

All you must do is follow the instructions in this kit and use common sense. You shouldn't need to hire a lawyer. However, if you find that your willmaking plans are more complicated than this kit allows, you may be interested in another self-help resource to accommodate your needs. (See the back of this booklet for a description of resources available from Nolo Press.)

To use this kit most efficiently, follow these seven steps:

Step 1. Read the overview (pages 4 through 6).

Step 2. Select the will form most appropriate for you.

Step 3. Carefully follow the step-by-step instructions.

Step 4. Make a rough draft of your will using an extra blank copy of the will form, provided in Appendix D of this booklet.

Step 5. Check your work. Then neatly type or print a final version of your will.

Step 6. Sign and date your will in front of two witnesses. (Three witnesses are required in Vermont.) Have the witnesses sign and date your will in the appropriate blanks.

Step 7. Store your will in a safe place.

LOOK FOR THESE ICONS

 A caution about potential problems.

 "Fast track" lets you know that you may be able to skip some material.

WHEN NOT TO USE THIS KIT

Preparing your own will is ordinarily a simple and straightforward process. In some circumstances, however, a will kit may not be the wisest route. The chart below flags those potential problem situations and recommends where to get help.

---

[1] Louisiana has unique laws governing wills.

WHEN YOU NEED HELP BEYOND THIS KIT

Seek additional help if...	Explanation	Where to get help
your net worth is at least $600,000	Hefty federal estate taxes come into play for estates worth $625,000 or more., depending or the year of death. A comprehensive estate plan can ensure that your beneficiaries will receive the maximum amount possible. (For an overview of estate planning, see pages 5 and 6)	See a lawyer or for more in-depth information on this subject, see *Plan Your Estate,* by Denis Clifford (Nolo Press).
you want to put restrictions on your inheritors	You can't use this will kit to place conditions on your property or beneficiaries. For example, you can't give property to one person to use during life, then require her to pass it to someone else. Or, you can't leave money to someone on condition that he go to college or change his religion.	See a lawyer.
you want to leave money or property to someone who can't manage his or her own finances	If your beneficiaries are financially irresponsible, physically disabled or emotionally disadvantaged, you might want someone else to oversee their property and make sure it is spent and managed in their best interests. Special types of trusts can be set up to accomplish that.	See a lawyer.
you think someone will object to your will	Most wills aren't contested. Don't use this kit, however, if you have reason to believe that your spouse, child or any other person is likely to object to your will.	See a lawyer.
you want to use your will to give away complex business interests	You can use this kit to give away business interests if that isn't prohibited by a contract, such as a partnership agreement. But to make an efficient transition from one owner to the next, you're probably better off using a living trust or making other arrangements.	See a lawyer or for more information on living trusts, see *Make Your Own Living Trust,* by Denis Clifford (Nolo Press).
you're married and you don't want to leave much to your spouse	Only use this kit if you plan to leave your spouse at least half of your estate. Most state laws guarantee a spouse one-third to one-half of the deceased spouse's property.	See a lawyer.

WILLS—AN OVERVIEW

To correctly prepare your own will, you'll need to learn a few legal concepts and a little legal terminology.

What Is a Will?

A **will** is a legal document in which you can:

- specify how you want everything you own to be distributed after you die
- name a trusted person to make sure your wishes are carried out, and
- name someone to care for your minor children and any property they inherit.

A will that is valid in the state where it is made is also valid in all other states.

Who Can Make a Will?

There are a few legal restrictions on the person creating a will.

Age Requirements. To make a will, you must be at least 18 years of age (19 years of age if you live in Wyoming or 14 years of age if you live in Georgia). In addition, some states allow younger people to make a will if they are married, in the military or are legally emancipated (have achieved adult status by order of a court).

Mental State. You must be of sound mind to prepare a valid will. That means you must:

- know what a will is, what it does and that you are making one
- understand the relationship between yourself and those you would normally provide for in your will, such as a spouse or children, and
- understand the kind and quantity of property you own and how to distribute it.

How To Leave Property by Will

The heart of a will describes how you want your property distributed after your death. The people and organizations you choose to receive your property are your **beneficiaries**.

Specific Bequests

If you want to leave specifically identified property to named beneficiaries, you'll make **specific bequests**. A specific bequest is a gift of named property—for example, a house, cash, heirlooms or a photo album.

Your first choices to receive property left in specific bequests are your **primary beneficiaries**. You can choose one person or organization for each specific bequest or you can name two or more to share the property.

> **Example:** Ken wants to make several specific bequests. He wants to leave his house, car and bank accounts to his wife, Gertrude. He wants to leave his art collection to his friend Ann. He wants to leave his books equally to his brothers, Jim and Michael. And he wants his daughter, Leslie, to inherit 60% of his vacation home and his son, Peter, to inherit 40%.

The bequests you make using wills in this kit specify a 45-day **survivorship period**. That means that a beneficiary must outlive you by at least 45 days—the minimum amount of time it usually takes to turn over property to a beneficiary. If you specify that the property is to go to one primary beneficiary and he or she dies before the survivorship period ends, the property will go to the **alternate beneficiary** you've selected. If the property is to be shared by two or more primary beneficiaries, a deceased primary beneficiary's share will go equally to the surviving primary beneficiaries; but if all of the primary beneficiaries don't survive you by 45 days, the property goes to the alternate beneficiary.

> **Example:** Maureen chooses her brothers, Larry, Charlie and Morris, as equal primary beneficiaries of an apartment building she owns. She chooses her daughter, Elise, as the alternate beneficiary of the building. Maureen and her three brothers are in a car accident; Maureen and Larry die instantly. Charlie and Morris are then entitled to equal shares of the building. But Charlie dies a few days later, meaning Morris will get the entire apartment building. Morris must survive 45 days after Maureen's death; if he does not, the building will go to Elise.

Residuary Estate

Your **residuary estate** consists of all property you own at your death except for:

- property you've left in specific bequests to named beneficiaries and alternates, and
- property you've arranged to pass outside of your will.

Your residuary estate includes property you overlook when making your will and property that comes into your hands after you make your will. Your residuary estate also includes property left in specific bequests that couldn't be distributed because neither the primary beneficiary nor alternate beneficiary survived you by 45 days.

If you make few specific bequests, your residuary estate can contain a great deal of property—the value of which can increase substantially from the time you write your will

If you make few specific bequests, your residuary estate can contain a great deal of property—the value of which can increase substantially from the time you write your will until the time you die. But it can also decrease in value because you spend or give away the property that would have been in it.

Your **residuary beneficiary**, who inherits your residuary estate, can be one or more people or organizations, including any of the people to whom you've left property in specific bequests. If none of your residuary beneficiaries survives you by 45 days, your residuary estate will pass to one or more people or organizations you've selected as the **alternate residuary beneficiary**.

> **Example:** Barbara makes specific bequests of cash to each of her children. She leaves the remainder of her property—her residuary estate—to her husband, Paul. She names her children as the alternative residuary beneficiaries, to inherit in equal shares. When Barbara dies, Paul will receive everything she owns, with the exception of the money left to her children. But if Paul doesn't outlive Barbara by 45 days, the children will receive their specified cash gifts plus equal shares of the residuary estate.

Wills, Probate and Estate Planning

Your **estate** is all the money and property you own at your death. The process of arranging for the transfer of property and providing for your loved ones after you die is called **estate planning**. Preparing a basic will is an essential step. Especially for larger estates, however, many more options are available. Estate planning normally includes transferring property during your lifetime to:

- reduce or limit death taxes
- control use of your estate by beneficiaries, and
- avoid probate.

Property that isn't passed under a will or through other arrangements, such as a joint tenancy or living trust, will be distributed according to your state's laws. Those laws divide property among a few close relatives according to set formulas, and completely exclude all friends and charities. (For an in-depth discussion of estate planning, see *Plan Your Estate,* by Denis Clifford (Nolo Press).)

Reducing Death Taxes

Estates of less than $625,000 to $1,000,000 depending on the year of death are exempt from federal estate taxes. All property left to a surviving spouse is also exempt, as long as that spouse is a U.S. citizen.

If either your estate alone, or the combined value of your own and your spouse's estate, exceeds $625,000, you may want to explore the possibility of planning to reduce your federal estate tax exposure. The main methods for doing this are special tax-savings trusts and giving some of the property away. Again, *Plan Your Estate* gives a good overview of this subject.

Estate Planning to Control Property

Most people are content to leave their property to others outright, and not try to control what they do with it. However, there are times when people want to impose controls on their property and those who get it. The usual solution is to create a trust imposing limits on how and when property may be used. For example, this may be a wise way to provide for someone with a physical or mental disability or who is otherwise unable to handle money. You'll likely need help from a lawyer to prepare these trusts.

Probate and Probate Avoidance

If you die with a valid will, the property you've left by will is distributed following a court process called **probate**. Probate is the legal process that includes filing a deceased person's will with a court, locating and gathering assets, paying off debts and death taxes and distributing what's left as the will directs. Some state laws permit a simplified probate process for small estates, which is relatively quick and inexpensive. But the usual probate process can take a long time and mount up costly lawyer's fees, which are often based on the value of the property. This generally means that the lower the value of the property passing through probate, the lower the probate fees are.

The main advantage to probate is that it gives creditors a deadline in which to file claims, often about four months. But probate often has serious drawbacks. It creates a public record and can be costly and tie up the property for a long time.

These disadvantages of probate prompt many people to use **probate-avoidance methods**—legal ways to leave property outside of their will so that it won't pass through the probate process. But if only a small amount of property will be subject to probate, going through hoops to avoid it usually isn't worth the bother. (See page 6 for a listing of the most common probate-avoidance methods.)

PROBATE-AVOIDANCE METHODS

The most common ways to pass property outside of probate are by using:

- **Pay-on-Death Bank Accounts.** You select someone to receive, at your death, any money remaining in your checking, savings or bank money market account or certificate of deposit. While you're alive, you can withdraw money from the account or change the beneficiary. These accounts are sometimes called "savings bank," "Totten trust" or "informal trust" accounts.

- **IRAs, Keoghs and Other Retirement Plans.** Many retirement plans—including IRAs and Keoghs—allow you to name a beneficiary to receive any funds remaining in the plan when you die.

- **Life Insurance.** Proceeds of a life insurance policy pass to its beneficiaries directly if a specific beneficiary is named. If, however, you designate your own estate as the policy beneficiary, the proceeds will be subject to probate.

- **Joint Tenancy and Tenancy by the Entirety.** Each joint tenant owns equal shares of property, such as a car, securities or a bank account. When one joint tenant dies, his or her share automatically goes to the surviving joint tenant(s). In some states, joint tenancy property held by a married couple is called "tenancy by the entirety."

- **Revocable Living Trusts.** You create this legal entity by preparing and signing a document that specifies whom you want to receive certain property at your death. During your lifetime, you retain full control over your property; you can change or revoke a revocable living trust for any reason. No trust income tax returns are required, and you don't have to maintain separate trust records.

- **Gifts Made During Your Lifetime.** Anything you give away while you are alive is not part of your estate when you die, so it is not subject to probate.

HOW TO FILL IN YOUR WILL FORM

Preparing a basic legal will is easy, as long as you follow the accompanying instructions carefully. Start by selecting the form that describes your situation, as set out in the chart below. (If you have any questions about your legal marital status, turn to page 8.)

Unmarried Couples Note: If you're a member of an unmarried couple, select a form for a single person. You can leave any property you wish to your partner. You can also name your partner as the executor of your will and the guardian of your children.

WHICH WILL FORM TO USE

Form	Use if you are...
WF-1	Single (or legally divorced) and have no children
WF-2	Single (or legally divorced) and have adult child(ren) only
WF-3	Single (or legally divorced) and have at least one minor child
WF-4	Married and have no children
WF-5	Married and have adult child(ren) only
WF-6	Married and have at least one minor child

The instructions in this section lead you through your will, line-by-line. One copy of each form is located in Appendix D. We suggest that you photocopy the form you need and use the copy to prepare a rough draft of your will. As you go along, you can also refer to the samples to see how your work will be incorporated into the final document.

Note: When you've finished your draft, you'll be able to prepare your final will by either:

• filling in the blanks on the will form, or

• retyping the will.

This issue is covered in more detail on page 23.

GUIDELINES FOR COMPLETING FORMS

• **Make your own will.** Each person is responsible for making his or her own willwriting decisions and signing his or her own will. Two or more people cannot sign the same will. If you need additional forms (for instance, you and your spouse are both preparing wills), photocopy the blank will forms before you fill them in.

• **Make a rough draft first.** Your final will must be prepared neatly and without mistakes. So start by preparing a draft of your document using an extra copy of the form you've selected, provided in Appendix D. After you've checked over your draft, you can transfer the information to a final will form or retype the will.

• **Cross out empty spaces.** Type or print lines or slash marks at the end of any clauses that you leave entirely or partially blank. That way, it'll be clear that you've skipped them intentionally.

Will Identification (Top of the Form)

Fill in your name in the blank after the words "Will of." Use the name you customarily use when you sign legal documents and other important papers. If you've used different names—for instance, you changed your name to Jerry Adams, but still own some property in the name of Jerry Adananossos—identify yourself with both names: "Jerry Adams, aka Jerry Adananossos." ("aka" stands for "also known as.")

In the next blanks, again fill in your name (or names), followed by your county, township or parish as well as your state. (If you have any doubt about your legal residence, see the information below.)

IDENTIFYING THE STATE YOU LIVE IN

Your state's laws affect a number of will-related issues such as marital property ownership, probate procedures and state inheritance taxes. The state of your legal residence is where you make your home now and for the indefinite future. You can have only one legal residence.

If you divide up the year by living in two or more states or you are temporarily residing outside the United States, choose as your state of residence the state in which you are the most rooted—for instance, where you:

• are registered to vote

• register your motor vehicles

• own real estate or other valuable property

• have checking, savings and other investment accounts

• maintain a business.

If you live overseas temporarily because you are in the Armed Services, your residence will be the Home of Record you declared to the military authorities.

1. Revocation

This standard language revokes (invalidates) all previous wills, including any handwritten ones. A revocation clause helps prevent possible confusion or litigation over the validity of prior wills. A revocation clause is used whether or not you have made another will; you don't need to add anything to the form here.

 Destroy Old Wills. Destroy all copies of wills you have made earlier; don't rely solely on this revocation clause to make them invalid.

2. Marital Status

If you're single or legally divorced and not remarried, the will form you've selected states, "I am not married."

If you're married, fill in your spouse's name. Provide the name he or she uses on official documents, such as a driver's license, tax returns or bank accounts.

YOUR MARITAL STATUS IS IMPORTANT

Your marital status could affect how and to whom you can leave your property. For example, if you're separated but not yet divorced, your estranged spouse may have a right to inherit a third to half of what you own.

If you're in the process of divorcing or are planning to marry, it's fine to make a will now. But make sure you write your will over again after your marital status changes. (See page 28.)

If you are unsure whether you are married or single according to law, here are some tips:

- **Separation or Pending Divorce or Annulment.** You remain legally married until a court issues a formal decree of divorce or annulment, signed by a judge. This is true even if you and your spouse have filed for divorce or annulment, are legally separated as declared in a legal document or live apart for an extended time.

- **Common Law Marriages.** Common law marriages are recognized in: Alabama, Colorado, the District of Columbia, Florida, Georgia, Idaho, Iowa, Kansas, Montana, Ohio, Oklahoma, Pennsylvania, Rhode Island, South Carolina and Texas. In those states, an unmarried woman and man automatically become legally married if they live together and either hold themselves out to the public as being married or actually intend to be married to one another. The marriage will still be valid even if they later move to a different state. There is no such thing as a common law divorce; a formal divorce proceeding is necessary to end a marriage.

- **Same Sex Marriages.** No state legally recognizes marriages between people of the same sex—even where a religious ceremony has been performed.

3. Children

 If you don't have any children (you're using form WF-1 or WF-4), skip to "Specific Bequests," page 10.

If you have children (you're using form WF-2, WF-3, WF-5 or WF-6), this listing in your will shows that you didn't inadvertently overlook any of them when you were making your will, which might automatically entitle them to a share of your estate.

List all of your natural born and adopted children, and any children born while you were not married. Do not list stepchildren unless you have gone to court and legally adopted them.

If you have any children who have died, their children may have the same protection against being accidentally overlooked as your own children. List all of your grandchildren if their parent (your child) has died. Also fill in the word "grandchild" in parentheses following each grandchild's name. You don't need to list children of children who are still living.

Will

of

Maria Gomez

I, ____Maria Gomez——,
a resident of _Kings County———————————_, State of _New York———————————_,
declare that this is my will.

1. **Revocation.** I revoke all wills that I have previously made.

2. **Marital Status.** I am not married.

3. **Children.** I have the following children:

Name	Date of Birth
Antonio Gomez	9-4-76
Juan Gomez	11-18-77
Delores Rivera (grandchild)	10-5-90
———	—
———	—

4. **Specific Bequests.** I make the following specific bequests of property:

I give _my house, located at 1501 Main Drive, New York, New York, and_
all household furnishings in it——————————————————————————————————
_——_
to _Rita Smith——_
or, if such beneficiary(ies) do(es) not survive me by 45 days, to __Consuela Hernandez——————_
_——._

I give _my dog Fifi and my 1992 Honda Accord, license #1992——————————_
_——_
_——_
to _Consuela Hernandez——_
or, if such beneficiary(ies) do(es) not survive me by 45 days, to _Rita Smith——————————_
_——._

I give _my unimproved lot located behind the Graham's farm in Solon,_
Ohio——
_——_
to _Antonio Gomez and Juan Gomez, in equal shares_
or, if such beneficiary(ies) do(es) not survive me by 45 days, to _Miguel Gomez (50%), Jesus_
Gomez (25%) and Jose Gomez (25%)——————————————————————————————.

Page _1_ of _6_

_____ _____ _____ _____
witness's initials   witness's initials   witness's initials   testator's initials

WF-3

WILLS   9

4. Specific Bequests

➡️ If you don't want to make any specific bequests, that means that you want to leave all your property to one or a small group of bene- ficiaries, in equal or unequal shares. Cross out this entire section and skip to Residuary Estate (page 16). (If you have children, and weren't planning to leave them anything, see the caution at the top of page 12).

If you want to make specific bequests to different individuals and organizations, follow these four steps. (An explanation of specific bequests is on page 4.)

Step 1: Decide What You Want to Give Away

Using the accompanying list to help jog your memory, make a list of the money and property you want to leave in specific bequests. Everything you don't leave in a specific bequest will go to the person or organization you select as your residuary beneficiary, as explained on pages 4 and 5.

To help you organize your wishes, a Specific Bequests Worksheet is provided in Appendix D, for your conve- nience. Or you may prefer to make a list on a separate piece of paper.

Your specific bequests list can be as detailed or as gen- eral as you want. For instance, if you don't own much prop- erty, or plan to make only a few specific gifts, jot down the brief list that reflects those decisions.

If, however, you own a variety of property and wish to divide it among a number of people and organizations, you may want to carefully itemize everything you own of mone- tary or sentimental value. Some people find it helpful to go through their homes and papers and inventory all of their possessions.

Note About Pets: You can give your pets away in your will. You can't, however, leave money or property to pets outright. You also can't use your will to put legal requirements on your pet's care. It's common to leave a pet to a friend or family member who's willing to care for it, perhaps with money to help pay for the pet's care. You also might wish to write a separate letter setting out details of how you'd like the beneficiary to care for your pet. (See page 24.)

PROPERTY YOU MAY WANT TO LEAVE BY WILL

REAL ESTATE (land and items permanently attached to land)

Agricultural land	Mobile home
Boat/Marina dock space	Rental property
Condo	Time-share
Co-op	Undeveloped land
Duplex	Vacation house
House	

PERSONAL PROPERTY (property other than real estate)

Animals	Letters, documents, papers
Antiques	Medals, awards, trophies
Appliances	Musical instruments
Art	Pets
Bank and cash accounts:	Photographs
Certificates of deposit	Precious metals
Checking accounts	Promissory notes, debts owed to you
Money market funds	Religious items, artifacts
Savings accounts	Royalties
Bicycles	Safe deposit contents
Books	Securities:
Business interests	Bonds
Cameras, photographic and video equipment	Commodities
	Mutual funds
China, crystal, silver	Stocks
Clothing, furs	Sentimental items
Coins, stamps	Small businesses
Collectibles (records, dolls, baseball cards, etc.)	Sports equipment
	Tools
Computer equipment	U.S. bills, notes and bonds
Copyrights, patents, trademarks	Vehicles, boats, aircraft:
Electronic equipment	Airplanes
Family heirlooms	Automobiles
Furniture	Boats
Hobbies	Motorcycles
Household furnishings	Motor homes/RVs
Inheritances	Watches
Jewelry	Wedding and engagement rings

Step 2: Identify Property You Don't Have the Right to Give Away

For some people, especially those with very little property and simple plans for leaving it, the laws that may affect property ownership simply do not affect their willmaking plans.

Example: Abigail wants to leave a few sentimental items to her friend Daniel. She wants her family photo albums to go to her sister, Linda. She plans to leave the rest of her property to her companion, Ellen, who co-owns everything valuable anyhow.

On the other hand, if you own valuable property jointly or own property that will pass outside of your will, such as a pay-on-death bank account, knowing exactly what you are entitled to give away may be very important to you, especially if you are trying to be even-handed in your requests.

Example: Avram is a widower. He and his brother own a house together. Avram wants to leave large gifts to his son, Ben, and his daughter, Freida. Avram plans to leave Ben a large gift of cash. He considers leaving Freida his half of the house. As it turns out, because of the way the property is owned (joint tenancy), Avram's brother automatically owns his half if he dies first. If Avram uses his will to leave his share of the house to Freida, she won't be entitled to it, meaning Ben would get cash and Freida would get nothing. Avram decides to leave both Ben and Freida large cash gifts.

 Skip to Step 3 on page 12 if you're not concerned about property ownership matters.

OWNERSHIP ISSUES THAT AFFECT PROPERTY LEFT BY WILL

Type of Ownership	Problem With Leaving It by Will	Where to Get More Information
Co-owned property, including real estate, cars, securities, small businesses, copyrights and other property	If you co-own property with someone else, you should determine how much you own and whether you have the right to give it away. You can't use your will to leave property that doesn't belong to you.	See Appendix A.
Marital (co-owned) property	Your spouse might be entitled to some of the property you own with him or her. If, however, you're leaving your share of that property to your spouse, you don't need to be concerned about property ownership rules.	See: • Appendix B if you live in Arizona, California, Idaho, Nevada, New Mexico, Texas, Washington or Wisconsin, or • Appendix C if you live in any of the other states.
Property with named beneficiaries, including: • life insurance • retirement plans • bank and security accounts • living trusts	If you've already named a beneficiary to receive any of this money or property, it will be distributed to that beneficiary, not to the person you name in your will.	Check with the institution handling the property if you want to change the beneficiary. (For information on living trusts, see *Plan Your Estate*.)
Property controlled by a contract, including: • partnership interests • stock in a small corporation controlled by shareholder approval	If there's a conflict over who gets this property at your death, the contract has preference over your will.	See a lawyer if you want to do something different in your will that conflicts with provisions in a contract.

Step 3:   Choose Who Will Receive Property Left in Specific Bequests

Your next step is to decide who gets what. Pages 4 through 5 describe how your property will be distributed after your death under this will.

⚠️ **Importance of Leaving Something to Children:** We strongly recommend that you name each of your children to receive a least some property under your will—even $1.00 will do. This same advice applies to the children of any of your children who are deceased (your grandchildren). The reason for this advice is to prevent a situation where a probate court second-guesses your intentions and awards a child a substantial portion of your estate on the ground that you would have wanted that result had you thought about it.

Select Primary Beneficiaries. For each item you wish to give in a specific bequest, choose the primary beneficiary (or beneficiaries)—your first choice to receive the property. You may name one or more people or organizations.

If you make any shared bequests, specify the percentage each beneficiary is to receive. If you don't specify percentages, the beneficiaries will share the property equally.

Example: Maria wants to leave several unshared bequests to individuals and organizations. She leaves her house and furnishings to her best friend, Rita and her dog and car to her sister, Consuela.

Maria also wants to leave several shared bequests. She leaves an unimproved parcel of land to her sons, Antonio and Juan, in equal shares. She leaves her art collection to her brother, Miguel, (60%) and her sister, Consuela (40%). Finally, she leaves her stock portfolio in equal shares to her three nephews, Raphael, Jesus and Jose. (Turn to pages 9 and 15 to see how Maria filled in her will.)

⚠️ **Problems With Shared Gifts.** Unless the property can easily be divided equally, leaving a bequest to more than one person to share can create problems down the line. For instance, if you leave all of your jewelry equally to your children, they may disagree about how to divide it or whether to sell it. (If you're determined to place controls on shared gifts to address these problems, you'll need to see a lawyer.)

Select Alternate Beneficiaries. For each specific bequest you've made, name one or more alternate beneficiaries—your second choice to receive the property. An alternate beneficiary will receive the property only if *all* primary beneficiaries for that specific bequest don't outlive you by at least 45 days. If you name two or more alternate beneficiaries, specify the percentage each is to receive.

Example: Maria leaves her house and furnishings to Rita. If Rita does not survive Maria by 45 days, Maria wants her sister, Consuela to inherit the house. (Look at the first specific bequest on page 9 to see how Maria filled in her will.)

NAMING DIFFERENT ALTERNATIVE BENEFICIARIES FOR SHARED GIFTS

If you leave a shared bequest and one of the beneficiaries doesn't outlive you by 45 days, all surviving beneficiaries will receive the deceased person's portion in equal shares.

But if you want a predeceased beneficiary's share to go instead to someone other than the remaining beneficiaries, it's easy to arrange. Simply split up portions of a bequest so you make separate single-item gifts. Then select alternate beneficiaries for each separate bequest.

Example: Maria wants to leave her cabin to her two sons, Antonio and Juan, and her sister, Consuela. She wants each son to receive a 40% share and her sister a 20% share. In the event one son does not survive her by 45 days, she wants his share to go to the surviving son. If her sister predeceases her, Maria wants that 20% share to pass to her brother, Miguel, rather than to either of her sons. To accomplish her goals, Maria makes three separate specific bequests:

40% share in cabin:	Primary beneficiary—Antonio Alternate beneficiary—Juan
40% share in cabin:	Primary beneficiary—Juan Alternate beneficiary—Antonio
20% share in cabin:	Primary beneficiary—Consuela Alternate beneficiary—Miguel

(Turn to page 15 and look at the last three specific bequests to see how Maria filled in her will.)

Step 4: Fill in Specific Bequests Clauses on Will Form

Depending on which will form you use, there is room for nine to ten specific bequests. If you make more specific bequests than a form allows, use an extra specific bequests sheet (form WF-SB). Or you could retype your entire will. If you make fewer specific bequests than a form allows, cross out the extra paragraphs (see the sample on page 15).

Fill in each of the blanks following the guidelines below.

Description of Property

You'll describe the property you want to give away in each specific bequest in the blanks after the words "I give."

There are no rules that require your property be listed in any particular form or legal language. You need only identify the property in sufficient detail so that there can be no question as to what you intended to give. Here are some tips.

- **Multiple gifts to the same beneficiaries.** It is fine to give a number of items in one blank, as long as the items are all going to the same primary and alternate beneficiaries: "my Rolex watch, skis and coin collection," "my dog, Gustav, my computer equipment and all my software."

- **Real estate.** Identify a home or business by its street address: "my condominium at 123 45th Avenue, San Francisco, California," or "my summer home at 84 Memory Lane, Oakville, Nevada." For unimproved (empty) land, use the name by which it is commonly known: "my undeveloped 10-acre lot next to the McHenry Place on Old Farm Road, Sandusky, Ohio." You don't need to give the legal description from the deed.

Real estate often includes items other than land and buildings. For instance, a farm may be given away with tools and animals and a vacation home may be given away with household furnishings. If you intend to keep both together as a gift, state that—for example, "my cabin at the end of Fish Creek Road in Wilson, Wyoming and all household furnishings and possessions in the cabin."

- **Bank and other financial accounts.** List financial accounts by their account numbers. Include the name and location of the institution holding the property: "Savings account #22222 at Independence Bank, Big Mountain, Idaho," "my money market account #2345 at Beryl Pynch & Company, Chicago, Illinois."

- **Personal and household items.** Separately identify any items and possessions with great emotional or financial value—a photo album, a cat or dog, an antique or work of art. If you own personal possessions you don't want to bother itemizing, list them in categories: "all my tools," "all my dolls," "all my baseball cards, records, machines and equipment," "all my personal possessions" or "all household furnishings and possessions in my house at 55 Drury Lane, Rochester, New York."

Primary Beneficiaries

List the primary beneficiaries who will receive each specific bequest of property in the blank following the word "to." For shared bequests, list all of the primary beneficiaries' names. If you want the primary beneficiaries to receive unequal shares, indicate the percentage each beneficiary is to receive in parentheses after each of their names. If you don't specify a percentage, the beneficiaries will share the property equally.

To ensure that your property will go to the people or organizations you want to get it, you must list them correctly. Don't use terms such as "all my children," "my surviving children," "my lawful heirs," or "my issue." If you use broad or vague terms, it may lead to serious interpretation problems when you are not there to explain what you mean.

Here are some guidelines on listing beneficiaries.

- **Naming organizations.** If you name a charity or a public or private institution, obtain the organization's complete name. Several different organizations may use similar names—and you want to be sure your gift goes to the correct organization.

- **Naming an individual.** List the full name by which the person is commonly known. This need not be the name that appears on a birth certificate, but it should clearly identify the person.

- **Shared gifts.** Name each person or organization who will receive the gift and specify how it should be divided. You can leave the gift equally or you can divide ownership up in any way you decide. Make sure your numbers add up to 100%.

- **Gifts to a couple.** If you want the gift to go to both members of a couple, list both of their names. If you list only one person, it will become that person's separate property. Indicate what percentage each member of the couple is to receive.

- **Gifts to minor children.** If the minor is your child, list him or her as a beneficiary. Later you will have the opportunity to provide for supervision of that property until your child reaches an age you choose. If the minor is not your child, you might consider leaving the gift to an adult you trust will use it for the child's benefit. The advantage of having an adult manage the gift is that no formal supervision—no court proceeding or recordkeeping of any kind—is required.

> ⚠️ **Legal Reality of Leaving Gift for an Adult to Supervise.** If you make a gift in your will to an adult with the understanding that it is for the benefit of a minor child, make sure you completely trust that adult. The adult is under no legal obligation to use the money or property for the child under this type of arrangement, only a moral one. (See page 26 for a discussion of how to spell out your wishes in a letter.)

Alternate Beneficiaries

In the last blank of each specific bequest, after the words "do(es) not survive me by 45 days, to," write in your alternate beneficiaries for each gift. Follow the guidelines above for naming primary beneficiaries and establishing percentages if two or more beneficiaries are to share a bequest.

The last part of this section of your will—after all the specific bequests and beneficiaries are listed—states that shared specific bequests are to be divided equally, unless specified otherwise. It also explains that a deceased beneficiary's share of property will be shared equally by surviving beneficiaries.

I give my art collection--

----

to Miguel Gomez (60%) and Consuela Hernandez (40%)-----------------------

or, if such beneficiary(ies) do(es) not survive me by 45 days, to Antonio Gomez and Juan

Gomez in equal shares-- .

    I give my stocks---

----

to Raphael Gomez, Jesus Gomez and Jose Gomez in equal shares-----------

or, if such beneficiary(ies) do(es) not survive me by 45 days, to Miguel Gomez, Antonio

Gomez, Juan Gomez and Consuela Hernandez in equal shares------------- .

    I give a 40% share of my cabin at Lake Bonne, Minnesota-------------

----

----

to Antonio Gomez---

or, if such beneficiary(ies) do(es) not survive me by 45 days, to Juan Gomez----------------- .

    I give a 40% share of my cabin at Lake Bonne, Minnesota-------------

----

----

to Juan Gomez--

or, if such beneficiary(ies) do(es) not survive me by 45 days, to Antonio Gomez------------- .

    I give a 20% share of my cabin at Lake Bonne, Minnesota-------------

----

----

to Consuela Hernandez--

or, if such beneficiary(ies) do(es) not survive me by 45 days, to Miguel Gomez--------------

---.

    I give _____

----

to _____

or, if such beneficiary(ies) do(es) not survive me by 45 days, to ---------------------------

---.

witness's initials   witness's initials   witness's initials   testator's initials

5. Residuary Estate

Your residuary estate will consist of all property that does not pass under a specific bequest or that you have not passed through other estate planning methods. (See page 5 and 6 for a summary of those methods and pages 4 through 5 for more information on residuary estates.)

In the first blank, name one or more individuals and institutions to take your residuary estate. You are free to name here the primary or alternate beneficiaries you named to take specific bequests; it's up to you.

If you name more than one residuary beneficiary, decide whether you intend for them to share the residuary property equally. If so, you need only list their names—such as Cynthia Kassouf, George Cobb and Bonita Cobb. Each will get a one-third share. If you want them to take unequal shares, decide what percentage each should receive and make sure that the percentages add up to 100%. Then list the percentage after each name.

In the last blank, after the words, "do(es) not survive me by 45 days, to," specify at least one alternate residuary beneficiary following the guidelines set out just above for naming residuary beneficiaries.

The last part of this section states that a shared residuary bequest will be divided equally, unless spcified otherwise. It also explains that a deceased residuary beneficiary's share will be shared equally by surviving residuary beneficiaries.

Importance of an Alternate Residuary Beneficiary: If your residuary beneficiaries die before you, and you haven't named any alternate residuary beneficiaries, your residuary estate will be distributed according to state law. (The wisest route is to make a new will if any major beneficiary dies; see page 29.)

6. Executor

Your **executor** is the person you name in your will to have legal responsibility for carefully handling your property and distributing it as your will directs.

Under the wills in this kit, your executor will decide how your debts, probate fees and any estate taxes will be paid, following guidelines set by state law. In carrying out the provisions of your will, your executor will have the option of hiring an attorney to help with any required court procedures. Your executor should not be required to post bond—a financial guarantee that the estate would be reimbursed should the executor mismanage or steal estate property.

The person you name as executor must be at least 18 years of age unless:

- you live in Alabama, Alaska or Nebraska, where the executor must be at least 19 years old, or
- you live in Arkansas or Utah, where the age requirement is 21 years of age.

Choose only one person to serve at a time. Naming co-executors can result in all kinds of problems, especially if the co-executors disagree or don't communicate well.

Choose as your executor a responsible person whom you completely trust. You can also select an **alternate executor** to serve if your first choice cannot. Common choices for executors and alternates are spouses, adult children, siblings and close friends who are willing and able to do the job. It's fine to name someone who will receive property under your will. Discuss the undertaking first to make sure that the person you name is willing to take on the responsibility.

It's Best to Name In-State Executors. It will be easier and less expensive for your executor to handle your probate, real estate and other business transactions if he or she lives nearby. In addition, the probate court may require that a cash bond be posted by an executor who lives out-of-state, even if you provide in your will that this isn't necessary.

Fill in the name of the executor after the words "I name." If you want to name an alternate executor to serve if your first choice cannot, fill in that person's name after the words, "If that executor does not qualify or ceases to serve, I name." If you don't want to name an alternate executor, cross out the blank space.

The rest of this section sets out the authority you wish to give your executor; you don't need to add anything else. These are broad powers that the executor may exercise at his or her discretion in carrying out the terms of your will.

Any specific bequest made in this will to two or more beneficiaries shall be shared equally among them, unless unequal shares are specifically indicated.

If I name two or more primary beneficiaries to receive a specific gift of property and any of them do not survive me by 45 days, all surviving primary beneficiaries shall equally divide the deceased beneficiary's share. If I name two or more alternate beneficiaries to receive a specific gift of property and any of them do not survive me by 45 days, all surviving alternate beneficiaries shall equally divide the deceased alternate beneficiary's share.

5. **Residuary Estate.** I give my residuary estate, that is, the rest of my property not otherwise specifically and validly disposed of by this will or in any other manner, to __Delores Rivera, Antonio Gomez and Juan Gomez------------------------------------__ or, if such residuary beneficiary(ies) do(es) not survive me by 45 days, to __Consuela Hernandez, Raphael Gomez, Jesus Gomez, and Jose Gomez---__.

Any residuary bequest made in this will to two or more residuary beneficiaries shall be shared equally among them, unless unequal shares are specifically indicated.

If I name two or more residuary beneficiaries and any of them do not survive me by 45 days, all surviving residuary beneficiaries shall equally divide the deceased residuary beneficiary's share. If I name two or more alternate residuary beneficiaries to receive a specific gift of property and any of them do not survive me by 45 days, all surviving alternate residuary beneficiaries shall equally divide the deceased alternate residuary beneficiary's share.

6. **Executor.** I name __Rita Smith--__ as executor, to serve without bond.

If that executor does not qualify or ceases to serve, I name __Consuela Hernandez------------__ __--__ as executor, also to serve without bond.

I direct that my executor take all actions legally permissible to probate this will, including filing a petition in the appropriate court for the independent administration of my estate.

I grant to my executor the following powers, to be exercised as the executor deems to be in the best interests of my estate:

(1) To retain property, without liability for loss or depreciation resulting from such retention.

(2) To sell, lease or exchange property and to receive or administer the proceeds as a part of my estate.

(3) To vote stock, convert bonds, notes, stocks or other securities belonging to my estate into other securities, and to exercise all other rights and privileges of a person owning similar property.

(4) To deal with and settle claims in favor of or against my estate.

(5) To continue, maintain, operate or participate in any business which is a part of my estate, and to incorporate, dissolve or otherwise change the form of organization of the business.

(6) To pay all debts and taxes that may be assessed against my estate, as provided under state law.

(7) To do all other acts, which in the executor's judgment may be necessary or appropriate for the proper and advantageous management, investment and distribution of my estate.

Page _3_ of _6_

WF-3

_____ witness's initials   _____ witness's initials   _____ witness's initials   _____ testator's initials

WILLS   17

7. Personal Guardian

 If you have no minor children (you're using form WF-1, WF-2, WF-4 or WF-5), skip to "Preparing, Signing and Storing Your Will," on page 23.

If you have minor children (you're using form WF-3 or WF-6), you must name someone to care for them should you and their other parent both die before the children become adults.

If you die before your children's other biological or adoptive parent,[2] that other parent normally has the legal right to assume sole custody. This is true if the parents are married, divorced, or never married.

If there's no parent available who's able and willing to do the job, some other adult must take responsibility for raising the minor children.[3] This adult is called a child's **personal guardian**. A personal guardian may be named in a will, but a judge selects the personal guardian in a court proceeding. Assuming the child's other parent isn't available, a deceased parent's choice of guardian is usually appointed, unless someone proves that choice of guardian wouldn't be in a child's best interest.

In your will, you name a person to serve as personal guardian for your children.[4] You can also name an **alternate personal guardian**, in case the first choice can't serve; if you don't want to name an alternate personal guardian, cross out that space.

When choosing a personal guardian and alternate, follow these guidelines:

- Select someone who is at least 18 years of age (21 years of age if you live in Colorado).
- Don't try to coerce someone to take on the responsibility of raising your kids. Be sure any person you name is ready, willing and able to do the job.
- If two parents are involved, they should agree on the person they want to appoint to take over if they die simultaneously.

---

[2]"Adoptive" refers to people who have legally adopted a child through a court proceeding, not people functioning as stepparents.

[3]An exception is the rare case where a minor is legally emancipated—that is, has been declared by a court to have achieved legal adult status.

[4]Legally, you can name different people as guardians. But the wills in this kit provide that all of your minor children will be supervised by the same person.

- It's best not to name joint personal guardians, even if two people will contribute to the child-rearing. Doing this raises many potential problems, especially if the couple splits up.
- You don't need to name your child's other parent; you may, however, wish to name a stepparent.

 If You Don't Want the Other Parent to Have Custody: A will won't prevent a court from awarding custody of your minor children to their other parent. If you die before your children reach adulthood, the children's other parent (not a stepparent) will probably get custody. See a lawyer if that concerns you, especially if the other parent has abandoned the children or you believe he or she is an unfit parent. You can document your claims now. You can also make arrangements for others to pursue custody if you die while your children are minors.

Fill in the name of the personal guardian after the words, "If at my death any of my children are minors and a personal guardian is needed, I name." In the space after "If this person is unable or unwilling to serve as personal guardian, I name" you may write in the name of an alternate personal guardian, who would be eligible to serve if the first choice can't serve. If you don't want to name an alternate personal guardian, cross out that space.

8. Property Guardian

 If you do not have minor children (you're using form WF-1, WF-2, WF-4 or WF-5), skip to "Preparing, Signing and Storing Your Will," on page 23.

Minors cannot legally own property outright, free of adult supervision, beyond a minimal amount—in the $2,500 to $5,000 range, depending on the state. So if you have minor children (you're using form WF-3 or WF-6), you'll need to arrange for some adult to handle valuable property that your children own or inherit.

This kit allows you to arrange to have your minor children's property managed in two ways:

1. Set up a children's trust, which can only cover property you leave in your own will (discussed on page 20), and

2. Name someone to serve as **property guardian**, who manages:

- property you leave your minor children outside of your will, such as life insurance proceeds or a bank account trust, unless you make other management arrangements, and

These powers, authority and discretion are in addition to the powers, authority and discretion vested in an executor by operation of law, and may be exercised as often as deemed necessary, without approval by any court in any jurisdiction.

7. **Personal Guardian.** If at my death any of my children are minors and a personal guardian is needed, I name

Consuela Hernandez--

as the personal guardian, to serve without bond.

If this person is unable or unwilling to serve as personal guardian, I name ___Raul Hernandez-----___ ------------------------------------ as personal guardian, also to serve without bond.

8. **Property Guardian.** If any of my children are minors and a property guardian is needed, I name _____ Consuela Hernandez--------------------- as the property guardian, to serve without bond.

If this person is unable or unwilling to serve as property guardian, I name ___Raul Hernandez-----___ ------------------------------------ as property guardian, also to serve without bond.

9. **Children's Trust.** All property I give in this will to any of the children listed in Section A, below, shall be held for each of them in a separate trust, administered according to the following terms:

A. Trust Beneficiaries and Age Limits

Each trust shall end when the following beneficiaries become 35, except as otherwise specified in this section.

Trust Beneficiary	Trust Shall End At Age
Antonio Gomez	21
Juan Gomez	25
--	------
--	------
--	------

B. Trustees

I name ___Consuela Hernandez---------------------___ as trustee, to serve without bond.

If this person is unable or unwilling to serve as trustee, I name ___Raul Hernandez------------___ -- as trustee, also to serve without bond.

C. Beneficiary Provisions

(1) The trustee may distribute for the benefit of the beneficiary as much of the net income or principal of the trust as the trustee deems necessary for the beneficiary's health, support, maintenance and education. In deciding whether to make a distribution to the beneficiary, the trustee may take into account the beneficiary's other income, resources and sources of support.

(2) Any trust income that is not distributed to a beneficiary by the trustee shall be accumulated and added to the principal of the trust administered for that beneficiary.

D. Termination of Trust

The trust shall terminate when any of the following occurs:

(1) The beneficiary becomes the age specified in Paragraph A of this trust;

any property you leave your children in your will, unless you set up a children's trust (discussed on page 20).[5]

The property guardian may also manage property your minor children inherit from others, unless other property management arrangements are made or the children's other parent is available to supervise that property.

This kit requires that you name a property guardian for your minor children (even if you also choose to use a children's trust for property you leave your children in your will). Here's why. First, the guardian will stand at the ready in case anyone leaves property to your children while they are still minors. Second, a property guardian may be needed even if you want the surviving parent to manage your children's property—for example, an insurance company may require a property guardian be appointed before it will release funds.

Although you must name a property guardian in your will, the guardianship won't go into effect unless a property guardian is needed and someone files papers in court. The court almost always follows the deceased parent's recommendation, as long as that is in the children's best interest.

Once appointed, the property guardian supervises money and other property subject to the guardianship on the children's behalf. The guardian periodically reports to the court about the status of the property—what was spent and how much was earned. The property guardian must seek court approval before selling valuable assets or making risky investments, such as investing in a start-up company. The property guardian should not be required to post bond—a financial guarantee that the estate would be reimbursed should the property guardian mismanage or steal estate property.

Choose a trusted person over 18 years of age (21 years of age if you live in Colorado) to serve as your children's property guardian. It's best to select someone who is willing to take on the responsibility, handles money well and lives fairly close to you. Because of paperwork and court appearances, a guardian who lives far from your children is not a wise choice. Often, the sensible choices are your spouse, a stepparent or the person you named to be the children's personal guardian.

Fill in the name of the property guardian after the words, "If any of my children are minors and a property guardian is needed, I name." In the space after "If this person is unable or unwilling to serve as property guardian, I name," you may write in the name of an alternate property guardian, who would be eligible to serve if the first choice can't serve. If you don't want to name an alternate property guardian, cross out that space.

You Need Not Name the Child's Other Parent. If you don't want the property guardian to be the child's other parent, simply don't name him or her. If you don't get along or that parent isn't prudent with money, he or she probably isn't a very good choice.

9. Children's Trust

If you don't have minor children (you're using form WF-1, WF-2, WF-4 or WF-5), skip to "Preparing, Signing and Storing Your Will," on page 23.

If you have any minor children (you're using form WF-3 or WF-6), you have the option of setting up a children's trust in your will. The children's trust you create only applies to property you leave your minor children in your own will. Other property your minor children receive after your death must be managed through a property guardianship (see page 18) or some other estate planning method.

Here's how a children's trust works. You appoint an adult as **trustee**, who will be responsible for managing property you've left to your minor children by will. You may also appoint an **alternate trustee** in case your first choice can't serve. If your children are minors when you die, the trustee will manage the property. Unless the property is worth very little, the trustee will transfer all property into a trust, manage the property and file separate state and federal tax returns for the trust.

If your children don't stand to get enough property to warrant a children's trust (less than $2,500 to $5,000 depending on the state), the trust won't have to be established. The person you'd named would just manage the property informally.

When You Don't Need a Children's Trust. If your children don't stand to receive anything valuable under your will as primary, alternate or residuary beneficiaries, you don't need to set up a children's trust. Cross out the blanks in this part of your will. Then skip to "Preparing, Signing and Storing Your Will," on page 23.

---

[5]It's usually wise for insurance proceeds or bank accounts to be turned over to an adult you designate to supervise them on your children's behalf. This arrangement bypasses the time-consuming and expensive property guardianship process. You'll need to prepare a written authorization; check with your insurance agent or the financial institution handling your account.

A. Trust Beneficiaries and Age Limits

Under "Trust Beneficiary," write in the name of each of your minor children for whom you want to set up a trust. Use the same names that you listed on the first page of your will.

Directly across from each trust beneficiary's name, underneath "Trust Shall End At Age," fill in any age between 18 and 35 at which you want the child to receive property. There is no general rule that will direct you in choosing an age for a particular child to get whatever trust property has not been spent on the child's health, welfare and educational needs. Base your choice on:

- the amount of money involved
- how much control you would like to impose over it
- the beneficiary's likely level of maturity as a young adult, and
- whether the property you leave, such as rental property or a small business, needs sophisticated management that a young adult is unlikely to master.

⚠ **Don't Use This Trust for Children Who Have Problems Managing Money.** A children's trust is not a suitable way to provide for people who are financially irresponsible, physically disabled or emotionally disadvantaged. To set up flexible lifetime management arrangements, you'll need a lawyer's help.

When you have listed your children and ages the trust will end, draw a line or slashes in any unused blank space.

B. Trustees

The trustee you name in your will has considerable flexibility in managing property you leave your minor children by will. The trustee can spend trust money for the children's living needs and educational and medical expenses. The trustee must file separate income taxes for the trust. A court does not appoint or supervise a trustee.

Your choice for trustee and any alternate trustee should be at least 18 years of age (21 years of age if you live in Indiana). The trustee and alternate trustee should be financially responsible and willing to take on the job of managing and doling out the trust property. If possible, they should live in your state, or geographically close; someone who lives far away may have problems managing a trust. You could select your children's other parent as trustee—however, that isn't legally required. The person you've selected as property guardian also may be an excellent choice for trustee or alternate trustee.

Fill in the name of the trustee after the words "I name." If you want to name an alternate trustee, fill in that person's name after the words, "If this person is unable or unwilling to serve as trustee, I name." If you don't want to name an alternate trustee, cross out the blank space.

The rest of this section sets out the terms of the trust; you don't need to add anything. Section C directs the trustee to use trust funds for the benefit of the trust beneficiaries, as the trustee sees fit, and to add any unspent income to the trust. Section D provides that trust property will pass to the trust beneficiaries when they reach the age you specified. If they die before reaching that age, the trust property will pass to their heirs. Sections E and F give the trustee broad discretionary powers to manage the trust property.

The trustee may hire accountants, lawyers, investment advisors and other assistants. The trustee may also choose to be paid out of the trust property or income.

Date, Signature and Witnesses

Leave the date, signature and witness lines blank for now. Detailed instructions are below.

(2) The beneficiary dies before becoming the age specified in Paragraph A of this trust;

(3) The trust property is used up through distributions allowed under these provisions.

If the trust terminates because the beneficiary reaches the specified age, the remaining principal and accumulated net income of the trust shall pass to the beneficiary. If the trust terminates because the beneficiary dies, the remaining principal and accumulated net income of the trust shall pass to the trust beneficiary's heirs.

E. Powers of Trustee

In addition to other powers granted to the trustee in this will, the trustee shall have:

(1) All the powers generally conferred on trustees by the laws of the state having jurisdiction over this trust;

(2) With respect to property in the trust, the powers conferred by this will on the executor; and

(3) The authority to hire and pay from the trust assets the reasonable fees of investment advisors, accountants, tax advisors, agents, attorneys and other assistants to administer the trust and manage any trust asset and for any litigation affecting the trust.

F. Trust Administration Provisions

(1) This trust shall be administered independent of court supervision to the maximum extent possible under the laws of the state having jurisdiction over this trust.

(2) The interests of trust beneficiaries shall not be transferable by voluntary or involuntary assignment or by operation of law and shall be free from the claims of creditors and from attachment, execution, bankruptcy or other legal process to the fullest extent permissible by law.

(3) Any trustee serving shall be entitled to reasonable compensation out of the trust assets for ordinary and extraordinary services, and for all services in connection with the complete or partial termination of any trust created by this will.

(4) The invalidity of any provision of this trust instrument shall not affect the validity of the remaining provisions.

I subscribe my name to this will this _____ day of _____, 19 _____, at

_____, State of _____,

and declare it is my last will, that I sign it willingly, that I execute it as my free and voluntary act for the purposes expressed, and that I am of the age of majority or otherwise legally empowered to make a will and under no constraint or undue influence.

_____
signature

WITNESSES

On this _____ day of _____, 19 _____, the testator,

_____, declared to us, the undersigned, that this instrument was his or her will and requested us to act as witnesses to it. The testator signed this will in our presence, all of us being present at the same time. We now, at the testator's request, in the testator's presence, and in the

Page 5 of 6

WF-3

_____   _____   _____   _____
witness's initials   witness's initials   witness's initials   testator's initials

PREPARING, SIGNING AND STORING YOUR WILL

Carefully follow the procedures set out below for preparing, signing and witnessing your will. If you neglect to take these steps, your will may be invalid.

Double-Check Your Draft Will

Look over your draft will and make sure it expresses your intentions. If you want to make any changes, do that now, so that you can include them in your final will.

⚠ **Be Sure to Provide for Your Spouse and Children.** If you're married, make sure you've left at least half of your property to your spouse. If you have children, make sure you've left something to each as a primary or alternate beneficiary of a specific or residuary bequest. (See the caution at the top of page 12 for a discussion of leaving gifts to your children.)

Prepare Your Final Will

Check that you've selected the right form; the chart on page 7 lists the will forms available on this kit and who should use each of them. Double-check the form code in the lower left-hand corner of each page of your will form.

Select the way you wish to prepare your final will from the three methods set out below; they're all legal. When selecting a method, bear in mind that your will is an important legal document that must be presented to a court before your property is dispersed or your wishes followed. It is a matter of common sense that the neater and more "official-looking" your will looks, the less possibility of your survivors being hassled by a court questioning the document's validity. You can choose to:

- retype the entire will using a typewriter or word processor
- type the information onto the will form, or
- neatly hand-print the information onto the will form, using an ink pen.

Follow these guidelines when preparing your final will:

Step 1. **Photocopy the will form.** If you're transferring information onto a will form, make several photocopies of the form before you start. That way, you'll have extra copies if you make any mistakes or later want to revise your will.

Step 2. **Prepare your will neatly and correctly.** Do not cross out words or use correction fluid or cover-up tape.

Step 3. **Don't change the will form.** The preprinted will forms in this kit are legally valid. You risk creating a confusing or ineffective document if you change any preprinted language (with the exception of crossing out blanks, as directed in the instructions).

Step 4. **Don't worry about insignificant errors.** It's fine to leave typos or spelling errors, as long as it's obvious what you meant. But if a typo changes the intent of your will, redo the page on which it appears.

Step 5. **Cross out blank spaces you're not using.** If you're filling in a will form and you reach the end of a clause that has a lot of blank space, type or write in lines or slash marks at the end, so it's clear you're finished. If you don't use all of the blanks provided, cross out the ones you don't need. (See the samples on pages 15 and 19.)

Step 6. **Fill in page numbers.** At the bottom of each page, write or type in the page numbers—for example: "Page 1 of 6," "Page 2 of 6" and so on. (See the sample below.)

```
┌─────────────────────────────────┐
│                                 │
│        Page   1   of   6        │
│                                 │
└─────────────────────────────────┘
```

Signing and Witnessing Your Will

Witnesses must watch you sign your will, then sign their names below your signature. Unless your will is properly witnessed, it won't be valid.

You won't need to use a notary unless you make your will "self-proving"—an option available in most states. (See page 26.)

Select Qualified Witnesses

Three witnesses must see you sign your will if you live in Vermont. Two witnesses are required in all other states, but it's best to use three, if possible, because a witness may die or move away before the will is probated.

After your death, the witnesses must usually appear in court (in person or through an affidavit) to confirm that the document offered is actually your will and that you were of sound mind when you made it. In most states, you can usually avoid the need for your witnesses to appear if you also complete a self-proving affidavit. See "Self-Proving Option," page 26.)

Follow these guidelines when selecting your witnesses:

- If practicable, select three witnesses, even if only two are required.

- Choose people who are legally competent and over age 18.

- Do not select a beneficiary of your will as a witness. This is important; if you leave property to a witness, that person may be disqualified from inheriting.

- Do not select your spouse or any of your children as witnesses.

Sign Your Will in the Presence of Witnesses

When you're ready to sign your will, call your witnesses together in one place. They need not read your will and you need not read it to them. However, they must all be aware that you intend the document to be your will; explain to them that you want them to witness your will. Identify the document before them as your will.

You must date the will and sign it in the presence of your witnesses. In the blanks provided, fill in the day, month and year you are signing the will as well as the county, township or parish and state where you are signing it. Then sign in ink in the same form of your name you used in your will. For example, if you start your will with the name of Elissa T. James, sign your will the same way, not in another form, such as "E. T. James" or "Elissa Thelma James."

Next, double-check that the pages are numbered—for example, "Page 1 of 5." (See page 23 for a sample.) Then initial every page of your will in the space indicated ("testator's initials"). The purpose of initialing every page of a will is to protect against the remote chance that some evil-doer will remove a page from your will and substitute a fraudulent page after you die.

Once you've signed and initialed your will, ask your witnesses to date and sign it in ink with their normal signatures and fill in their addresses in the spaces indicated. Then ask the witnesses to initial each page of the will. If you don't want your witnesses to see what is in your will when they are initialing it, cover each page.

If Your Will Doesn't Say It All

 Skip to "Self-Proving Option," below, if you don't want to write a letter explaining any of your willwriting decisions.

You may have created a will that does exactly what you want it to, except that it does not explain why you've made

certain decisions. The best way to clarify your reasons to your beneficiaries is to prepare a separate letter and store it along with your will. (See the accompanying sample.)

Here are some examples of issues you may want to cover.

- **Pets.** You can't legally put requirements on how your pets will be cared for, but you can make your wishes known, especially if you've left money to help pay for their upkeep.

- **Unequal gifts.** If you've left more property to one person than another, you may want to explain why. For instance, parents might leave more money to a child who doesn't earn a lot, or less money to a child who has already received part of his or her inheritance.

- **Gifts to adults to use for children.** If you've left money or property to an adult, with the understanding that it's for the benefit of a child, you can clarify how you want the gift used. Although your wishes won't be legally binding, they'll go a long way in establishing that the money was for college, not a car.

- **Funeral arrangements.** You may want to express your wishes about your funeral, memorial service, cremation, burial or organ donation. Be sure to give a copy of these instructions to another person; wills are often not discovered and dealt with until long after decisions about final disposition have been made.

December 16, 1993

To My Executor:

This letter expresses my feelings and reasons for certain decisions made in my will. This letter is not my will, nor do I intend it to be an interpretation of my will. My will, which was signed by me, dated and witnessed on December 10, 1993, is the sole expression of my intentions concerning all my property, and other matters covered in it.

Should anything I say in this letter conflict with, or seem to conflict with, any provision of my will, the will provision shall be followed.

I request that my executor give a copy of this letter to each person mentioned in this letter, and to anyone else my executor determines should receive a copy.

I am giving the bulk of my property to my son John for one reason: because of his health problems, he needs it more. I love my other children, Ted and Ellen, just as much, and I am extremely proud of the life choices they have made. But the truth is that they can manage fine without a boost from me, and John can't.

Lee Monroe

These powers, authority and discretion are in addition to the powers, authority and discretion vested in an executor by operation of law, and may be exercised as often as deemed necessary, without approval by any court in any jurisdiction.

I subscribe my name to this will this _14th_ day of _December_ , 19 _9X_ , at _Hennepin County_ , State of _Minnesota_ , and declare it is my last will, that I sign it willingly, that I execute it as my free and voluntary act for the purposes expressed, and that I am of the age of majority or otherwise legally empowered to make a will and under no constraint or undue influence.

Sandi Browne
signature

WITNESSES

On this _14th_ day of _December_ ,19 _9X_ , the testator, _Sandi Browne_ , declared to us, the undersigned, that this instrument was his or her will and requested us to act as witnesses to it. The testator signed this will in our presence, all of us being present at the same time. We now, at the testator's request, in the testator's presence, and in the presence of each other, subscribe our names as witnesses and each declare that we are of sound mind and of proper age to witness a will. We further declare that we understand this to be the testator's will, and that to the best of our knowledge the testator is of the age of majority, or is otherwise legally empowered to make a will, and appears to be of sound mind and under no constraint or undue influence.

We declare under penalty of perjury that the foregoing is true and correct, this _14th_ day of _December_ , 19 _9X_ , at _Hennepin County_ , State of _Minnesota_ .

James Wilson	James Wilson
witness' signature	typed or printed name
residing at 8401 Maple Way	Minneapolis
street address	city
Hennepin	Minnesolta
county	state
Karen Wilson	Karen Wilson
witness' signature	typed or printed name
residing at 8401 Maple Way	Minneapolis
street address	city
Hennepin	Minnesolta
county	state
Michael McCoy	Michael McCoy
witness' signature	typed or printed name
residing at 22 Third Avenue	Minneapolis
street address	city
Hennepin	Minnesolta
county	state

Page _4_ of _4_   _JW_   _KW_   _MC_   _SB_
witness's initials   witness's initials   witness's initials   testator's initials

WF-1

Self-Proving Option

→ You cannot use the self-proving affidavits provided in this kit if you live in California (where a self-proving affidavit isn't required),[6] the District of Columbia, Maryland, Michigan, New Hampshire,[7] Ohio, Vermont or Wisconsin. If you live in one of these states, or you choose not to use the self-proving option, skip to "Copying Your Will" on page 28.

In all other states, you can potentially simplify the probate process if you and your witnesses sign a simple **self-proving affidavit** in front of a notary public. A self-proving affidavit, which is attached to your will and included in this kit, declares that the document is your will and that it was properly signed and witnessed. Self-proving your will doesn't affect its validity, it simply eliminates the requirement that a witness appear in person or file a written affidavit at the probate proceeding after your death.

Here's how to make your will self-proving.

Step 1. Sign your will and have it witnessed.

Step 2. Either have a notary present at the will signing or find a notary at a later time. Either way, you and your witnesses must personally appear together before the notary.

Step 3. Tell the notary that you want to make your will self-proving and ask whether he or she has a form for doing that. If so, use that form and follow the notary's instructions.

Step 4. If the notary doesn't have the form, select the correct form provided in Appendix D for your state. One copy of each form is included in Appendix D. (Only one sample is provided; all self-proving affidavits have similar wording.)

WHICH AFFIDAVIT TO USE

Form	Use if you live in...
Aff-1	Alabama, Alaska, Arizona, Arkansas, Colorado, Connecticut, Hawaii, Idaho, Illinois, Indiana, Maine, Minnesota, Mississippi, Montana, Nebraska, Nevada, New Mexico, New York, North Dakota, Oregon, South Carolina, South Dakota, Tennessee, Utah, Washington and West Virginia.
Aff-2	Delaware, Florida, Georgia, Iowa, Kansas, Kentucky, Massachusetts, Missouri, New Jersey, North Carolina, Oklahoma, Pennsylvania, Rhode Island, Virginia and Wyoming.
Aff-3	Texas

Step 5. Write your name and your witnesses' names and addresses in the spaces indicated in the affidavit and give the form to the notary. The notary will have you and your witnesses swear to the truth of the statement in the affidavit. The notary may require some identification from you and your witnesses, such as a driver's license, before signing and dating the affidavit and putting the notary seal on it.

Step 6. Staple the affidavit to your will. If you ever make a new will, also make a new affidavit.

⚠ **Reminder:** Both you and your witnesses must sign your will in addition to signing this affidavit. The affidavit and will are two separate documents.

---

[6]California residents don't need to prepare self-proving affidavits; the declaration contained in the will form that witnesses sign makes the will self-proving in California.

[7]New Hampshire allows self-proving of wills, but requires that special language be included as part of the will document, rather than on a separate form.

AFFIDAVIT

We, _Sandi Browne_ ,

James Wilson ,

Karen Wilson and

Michael McCoy , the

testator and the witnesses, whose names are signed to the attached instrument in those capacities, personally appearing before the undersigned authority and being first duly sworn, declare to the undersigned authority under penalty of perjury that:

1) the testator declared, signed and executed the instrument as his or her last will;

2) he or she signed it willingly or directed another to sign for him or her;

3) he or she executed it as his or her free and voluntary act for the purposes therein expressed; and

4) each of the witnesses, at the request of the testator, in his or her hearing and presence, and in the presence of each other, signed the will as witness and that to the best of his or her knowledge the testator was at that time of full legal age, of sound mind and under no constraint or undue influence.

Testator: _Sandi Browne_

Witness: _James Wilson_

Address: _8401 Maple Way, Minneapolis, MN_

Witness: _Karen Wilson_

Address: _8401 Maple Way, Minneapolis, MN_

Witness: _Michael McCoy_

Address: _22 Third Avenue, Minneapolis, MN_

Subscribed, sworn and acknowledged before me, _____ ,

a notary public, by _Sandi Browne_ ,

the testator, and by _James Wilson_ ,

Karen Wilson ,

and _Michael McCoy_ ,

the witnesses, this _14th_ day of _December_ , 19 _9X_ .

[NOTARY SEAL]

_____
Signature of notary public

My commission expires: _____

Copying Your Will

Don't prepare more than one signed and witnessed original of your will; if you later want to change your will, it can be difficult to locate all the old ones to destroy them.

You may, however, want to give an unsigned copy to your proposed executor and your spouse, friends or children. If you wish to keep the contents of your will confidential until your death, don't make and distribute copies.

Storing Your Will

Your will should be easy to locate at your death. You don't want your loved ones to undergo the anxiety of having to search for your will when they are already dealing with the grief of losing you. Here are some suggestions.

- Staple the pages of your will together. That will prevent any pages from getting lost or misplaced.

- Place your signed and witnessed will in an envelope on which you have typed or printed the words "Will of (Your Name)."

- If you've prepared a self-proving affidavit, make sure it's stapled to your will. If you've written any letters explaining your decisions and wishes, store them in the envelope with your will.

- Store the envelope in a fireproof metal box, file cabinet or home safe. A safe deposit box probably isn't the best place to store your will because your bank will probably limit access to the box after your death. In some states, such as Ohio and Texas, the local court clerk's office stores wills for a small fee; check with the clerk for details.

- Make sure your executor, and at least one other person you trust, know where to find your will.

KEEPING YOUR WILL UP-TO-DATE

Changes in your marital status, where you live, what property you own and whether you have children may affect what you include in your will. While not all life changes require that you also change your will, significant changes often do.

Changing Your Will

The laws of all states require that after a will is signed, any additions or changes to it, even correcting typos, must be made following the same signing and witnessing requirements as for an original will. The best way to make changes to a signed will is to make a new will. By making a new will, you revoke the old one.

When to Make a New Will

In some situations, you must make a new will or you risk invalidating your will or invalidating your wishes for how your property is distributed. Make a new will if:

- your marital status changes (even if you divorce and then remarry the same person)

- you adopt or have additional children

- a child or spouse dies.

Changes That May Require a New Will

In some situations, it's a good idea to make a new will. Consider writing a new will if:

- a major beneficiary dies

- you change your mind about to whom you want to leave your property

- the property you own changes significantly—for example, you sell your house or close all your bank accounts—and you made or want to make specific bequests

- a joint tenant dies, you haven't designated anyone to receive your share of the joint tenancy property and you wish to do so

- the person you named as executor is no longer able to serve

- the person you named as personal guardian for your minor children or manager for their property is no longer available to serve

- your witnesses move, die or are no longer competent (unless you've made your will self-proving), or

- you move to a different state.

How To Make a New Will

Follow the instructions in this kit to prepare a new will that reflects your current willwriting wishes. Destroy all old wills by tearing up or burning them.

APPENDICIES

If you own property with someone else, state laws may affect how you may leave your property. (If you are married, also see Appendix B if you live in a community property state or Appendix C if you live in a common law property state.)

Co-owned property may be held in one of these ways:

- tenancy in common
- joint tenancy, or
- tenancy by the entirety.

If you have a deed or other title document, the method of ownership will be listed there. (If the title document is confusing or unclear, check with the registrar of deeds, a title company or agency that monitors the title, such as the motor vehicles department.)

Tenancy in Common

This is a type of property ownership where owners hold either equal or unequal shares.

Rules for Leaving Property by Will

You are free to give away your share of property held in tenancy in common unless restricted by:

- marital ownership laws (see Appendices B and C)
- a contract—for example, a partnership agreement that restricts you from giving away your share, or
- a separate designation of beneficiaries—as is common for pay-on-death bank accounts, retirement plans and life insurance contracts.

Joint Tenancy

This type of property ownership is also called "joint tenancy with right of survivorship" or simply "with right of survivorship." A few states restrict what property can be held in joint tenancy, often limiting it to real estate.

When property is held in joint tenancy, all owners hold equal shares. When one owner dies, his or her share auto-matically goes to the surviving owners to share equally.

Rules for Leaving Property by Will

You cannot give away your share of joint tenancy property. It automatically goes to any surviving joint tenants in equal shares.

You may, however, include joint tenancy property in your will to account for the possibility that:

- the entire property ends up in your estate because the other joint tenants die before you, or
- the property is converted to tenancy in common. Any owner is permitted to change the way property is held simply by creating a new deed, title slip or other document.

Tenancy by the Entirety

This is a type of property ownership that is basically the same as joint tenancy discussed above, but it is limited to married couples in the following states:

*Alaska	Maryland	Ohio
Arkansas	Massachusetts	Oklahoma
Delaware	*Michigan	*Oregon
District of Columbia	Mississippi	Pennsylvania
Florida	Missouri	Tennessee
Hawaii	*New Jersey	Vermont
*Indiana	*New York	*Virginia
*Kentucky	*North Carolina	*Wyoming

*Allows tenancy by the entirety only for real estate.

Rules for Leaving Property by Will

You cannot give away your share of property held in tenancy by the entirety; your spouse automatically inherits it. You can, however, include this property in your will to account for the possibility that:

- the property ends up in your estate because your spouse dies before you, or
- the property is converted to tenancy in common. Any owner is permitted to change the way property is held simply by creating a new deed, title slip or other document.

APPENDIX B:
BASIC RULES FOR LEAVING PROPERTY BY WILL
FOR MARRIED PEOPLE IN COMMUNITY PROPERTY STATES

If you are married and live in one of the following eight states, the property you and your spouse own falls under community property rules:

Arizona   Nevada   Washington
California   New Mexico   Wisconsin
Idaho   Texas

(If you are married and live in any other state, turn to Appendix C.)

Property owned by spouses in community property states is classified as either:

- separate property, or
- community property.

Separate property

In community property states, separate property is owned by only one spouse. This consists of:

- property accumulated prior to marriage
- earnings, if the spouse who earns them keeps the earnings separate—with the exception of Washington, where earnings are always community property
- gifts or inheritances received during marriage, directed to only one spouse (wedding gifts are community property)
- property that, despite originally being classified as community property, is converted into separate property by gift or agreement (which must be written in some states)
- property acquired after legal separation
- property accumulated during marriage with premarital earnings or income (such as income from a pension that vested before marriage) or with the proceeds of the sale of premarital property, only in Arizona, California, Nevada, New Mexico or Washington. (If this point matters to you and you live in Wisconsin, see a lawyer.)

Rules for Leaving Property by Will

You can give away all of your separate property, unless:

- the property is held in joint tenancy (see Appendix A)
- the property has a separate designation of beneficiaries—as is common for pay-on-death bank accounts, retirement plans and life insurance contracts, or

- the property is restricted from transfer by a contract—for example, a partnership agreement that restricts you from giving away your share.

Community property

In community property states, community property is owned in equal shares by a married couple. This consists of:

- earnings received by either spouse during marriage. The primary exception to this rule is that all community property states except Washington allow spouses to treat earnings as the separate property of the spouse who earns them if that spouse keeps the income separate—as in a separate bank account to which the other spouse has no access
- property and income acquired with community earnings and income
- gifts made to both spouses (including wedding gifts)
- property that, despite originally being classified as separate property, gets mixed together—or "commingled"—with community property so that it's no longer possible to tell the difference between the two. This often happens when both spouses deposit their wages earned during marriage into an account containing one or both spouse's separate money
- property that, despite originally being classified as separate property, is deliberately turned into community property by the spouses. This commonly occurs when one spouse makes a gift of separate property to the community, such as transferring the title of a separately-owned home into both spouses' names (in some states, a separate written agreement may be required)
- income from separate property (defined above), only in Texas or Idaho. (If this point matters to you and you live in Wisconsin, see a lawyer.)

Rules for Leaving Property by Will

You can give away your half of community property, unless:

- the property is held in joint tenancy (see Appendix A)
- the property has a separate designation of beneficiaries—as is common for pay-on-death bank accounts, retirement plans and life insurance contracts , or
- the property is restricted from transfer by a contract—for example, a partnership agreement that restricts you from giving away your share.

APPENDIX C:
BASIC RULES FOR LEAVING PROPERTY BY WILL
FOR MARRIED PEOPLE IN COMMON LAW PROPERTY STATES

Common law property states are all states other than Arizona, California, Idaho, Nevada, New Mexico, Texas, Washington and Wisconsin. (See Appendix B if you live in one of those states.)

> ⚠️ **Warning.** Do not use this kit if you intend to leave your spouse less than half of your property. All common law property states have laws that ensure that a surviving spouse will receive a share—typically one-third to one-half of the deceased spouse's property.

Separate property

In common law property states, separate property is property that only one spouse owns. This consists of:

- property owned in one spouse's name
- property purchased with income or the proceeds of the sale of property held in only one spouse's name.

Rules for Leaving for Property by Will

You can give away all of your separate property, unless:

- the property is held in joint tenancy or tenancy by the entirety (see Appendix A)
- the property has a separate designation of beneficiaries—as is common for pay-on-death bank accounts, retirement plans and life insurance contracts, or
- the property is restricted from transfer by a contract—for example, a partnership agreement that restricts you from giving away your share.

Marital property

In common law property states, marital property is property that both spouses own together. This consists of:

- property held in both spouses' names
- property spouses purchased with income or the proceeds of the sale of property held in both spouses' names.

Rules for Leaving Property by Will

You can give away your share of jointly owned property, unless:

- the property is held in joint tenancy or tenancy by the entirety (see Appendix A)
- the property has a separate designation of beneficiaries—as is common for pay-on-death bank accounts, retirement plans and life insurance contracts, or
- the property is restricted from transfer by a contract—for example, a partnership agreement that restricts you from giving away your share.

APPENDIX D:
BLANK WILL FORMS

Will Forms	To be used by a person who is…
• **WF-1**	single (or legally divorced) and has no children
• **WF-2**	single (or legally divorced) and has adult child(ren) only
• **WF-3**	single (or legally divorced) and has at least one minor child
• **WF-4**	married and has no children
• **WF-5**	married and has adult child(ren) only
• **WF-6**	married and has at least one minor child

Specific Bequests Forms

- **Extra Specific Bequests (WF-SB)**
- **Specific Bequests Worksheet**

Self-Proving Affidavits	For use in…
• **Aff-1**	Alabama, Alaska, Arizona, Arkansas, Colorado, Connecticut, Hawaii, Idaho, Illinois, Indiana, Maine, Minnesota, Mississippi, Montana, Nebraska, Nevada, New Mexico, New York, North Dakota, Oregon, South Carolina, South Dakota, Tennessee, Utah, Washington and West Virginia
• **Aff-2**	Delaware, Florida, Georgia, Iowa, Kansas, Kentucky, Massachusetts, Missouri, New Jersey, North Carolina, Oklahoma, Pennsylvania, Rhode Island, Virginia and Wyoming
• **Aff-3**	Texas

Will

of

_____

I, _____ ,

a resident of _____ , State of _____ ,

declare that this is my will.

    1. **Revocation.** I revoke all wills that I have previously made.

    2. **Marital Status.** I am not married.

    3. **Children.** I do not have any children.

    4. **Specific Bequests.** I make the following specific bequests of property:

I give _____

_____

_____

to _____

or, if such beneficiary(ies) do(es) not survive me by 45 days, to _____

_____ .

    I give _____

_____

_____

to _____

or, if such beneficiary(ies) do(es) not survive me by 45 days, to _____

_____ .

    I give _____

_____

_____

to _____

or, if such beneficiary(ies) do(es) not survive me by 45 days, to _____

_____ .

    I give _____

_____

_____

to _____

or, if such beneficiary(ies) do(es) not survive me by 45 days, to _____

_____ .

_____   _____   _____   _____

  witness's initials   witness's initials   witness's initials   testator's initials

WF-1

I give _____

_____

_____

to _____

or, if such beneficiary(ies) do(es) not survive me by 45 days, to _____

_____ .

I give _____

_____

_____

to _____

or, if such beneficiary(ies) do(es) not survive me by 45 days, to _____

_____ .

I give _____

_____

_____

to _____

or, if such beneficiary(ies) do(es) not survive me by 45 days, to _____

_____ .

I give _____

_____

_____

to _____

or, if such beneficiary(ies) do(es) not survive me by 45 days, to _____

_____ .

I give _____

_____

_____

to _____

or, if such beneficiary(ies) do(es) not survive me by 45 days, to _____

_____ .

I give _____

_____

_____

to _____

or, if such beneficiary(ies) do(es) not survive me by 45 days, to _____

_____ .

| _____ | _____ | _____ | _____ |
| witness's initials | witness's initials | witness's initials | testator's initials |

WF-1

Any specific bequest made in this will to two or more beneficiaries shall be shared equally among them, unless unequal shares are specifically indicated.

If I name two or more primary beneficiaries to receive a specific gift of property and any of them do not survive me by 45 days, all surviving primary beneficiaries shall equally divide the deceased beneficiary's share. If I name two or more alternate beneficiaries to receive a specific gift of property and any of them do not survive me by 45 days, all surviving alternate beneficiaries shall equally divide the deceased alternate beneficiary's share.

5. **Residuary Estate.** I give my residuary estate, that is, the rest of my property not otherwise specifically and validly disposed of by this will or in any other manner, to _____ _____ or, if such residuary beneficiary(ies) do(es) not survive me by 45 days, to _____ _____ .

Any residuary bequest made in this will to two or more residuary beneficiaries shall be shared equally among them, unless unequal shares are specifically indicated.

If I name two or more residuary beneficiaries and any of them do not survive me by 45 days, all surviving residuary beneficiaries shall equally divide the deceased residuary beneficiary's share. If I name two or more alternate residuary beneficiaries to receive a specific gift of property and any of them do not survive me by 45 days, all surviving alternate residuary beneficiaries shall equally divide the deceased alternate residuary beneficiary's share.

6. **Executor.** I name _____ as executor, to serve without bond.

If that executor does not qualify or ceases to serve, I name_____ _____ as executor, also to serve without bond.

I direct that my executor take all actions legally permissible to probate this will, including filing a petition in the appropriate court for the independent administration of my estate.

I grant to my executor the following powers, to be exercised as the executor deems to be in the best interests of my estate:

(1) To retain property, without liability for loss or depreciation resulting from such retention.

(2) To sell, lease or exchange property and to receive or administer the proceeds as a part of my estate.

(3) To vote stock, convert bonds, notes, stocks or other securities belonging to my estate into other securities, and to exercise all other rights and privileges of a person owning similar property.

(4) To deal with and settle claims in favor of or against my estate.

(5) To continue, maintain, operate or participate in any business which is a part of my estate, and to incorporate, dissolve or otherwise change the form of organization of the business.

(6) To pay all debts and taxes that may be assessed against my estate, as provided under state law.

(7) To do all other acts, which in the executor's judgment may be necessary or appropriate for the proper and advantageous management, investment and distribution of my estate.

Page ___ of ___   _____   _____   _____   _____
witness's initials   witness's initials   witness's initials   testator's initials

WF-1

These powers, authority and discretion are in addition to the powers, authority and discretion vested in an executor by operation of law, and may be exercised as often as deemed necessary, without approval by any court in any jurisdiction.

I subscribe my name to this will this _____ day of _____, 19 _____ , at _____ , State of _____ , and declare it is my last will, that I sign it willingly, that I execute it as my free and voluntary act for the purposes expressed, and that I am of the age of majority or otherwise legally empowered to make a will and under no constraint or undue influence.

_____
signature

WITNESSES

On this _____ day of _____ ,19 _____ , the testator, _____ , declared to us, the undersigned, that this instrument was his or her will and requested us to act as witnesses to it. The testator signed this will in our presence, all of us being present at the same time. We now, at the testator's request, in the testator's presence, and in the presence of each other, subscribe our names as witnesses and each declare that we are of sound mind and of proper age to witness a will. We further declare that we understand this to be the testator's will, and that to the best of our knowledge the testator is of the age of majority, or is otherwise legally empowered to make a will, and appears to be of sound mind and under no constraint or undue influence.

We declare under penalty of perjury that the foregoing is true and correct, this _____ day of _____ , 19 _____ , at _____ , State of _____ .

_____   _____
            witness' signature   typed or printed name
residing at _____ , _____ ,
                        street address   city
_____ , _____ .
            county   state

_____   _____
            witness' signature   typed or printed name
residing at _____ , _____ ,
                        street address   city
_____ , _____ .
            county   state

_____   _____
            witness' signature   typed or printed name
residing at _____ , _____ ,
                        street address   city
_____ , _____ .
            county   state

Page ___ of ___   _____   _____   _____   _____
                   witness's initials witness's initials witness's initials   testator's initials

WF-1

Will

of

_____

I, _____ ,

a resident of _____ , State of _____ ,

declare that this is my will.

1. **Revocation.** I revoke all wills that I have previously made.

2. **Marital Status.** I am not married.

3. **Children.** I have the following children:

Name   Date of Birth
_____

4. **Specific Bequests.** I make the following specific bequests of property:

I give _____

_____

_____

to _____

or, if such beneficiary(ies) do(es) not survive me by 45 days, to _____

_____ .

I give _____

_____

_____

to _____

or, if such beneficiary(ies) do(es) not survive me by 45 days, to _____

_____ .

I give _____

_____

_____

to _____

or, if such beneficiary(ies) do(es) not survive me by 45 days, to _____

_____ .

_____   _____   _____   _____
witness's initials   witness's initials   witness's initials   testator's initials

WF-2

I give _____

_____

_____

to _____
or, if such beneficiary(ies) do(es) not survive me by 45 days, to _____

_____ .

I give _____

_____

_____

to _____
or, if such beneficiary(ies) do(es) not survive me by 45 days, to _____

_____ .

I give _____

_____

_____

to _____
or, if such beneficiary(ies) do(es) not survive me by 45 days, to _____

_____ .

I give _____

_____

_____

to _____
or, if such beneficiary(ies) do(es) not survive me by 45 days, to _____

_____ .

I give _____

_____

_____

to _____
or, if such beneficiary(ies) do(es) not survive me by 45 days, to _____

_____ .

I give _____

_____

_____

to _____
or, if such beneficiary(ies) do(es) not survive me by 45 days, to _____

_____ .

Page ___ of ___   _____   _____   _____   _____
                    witness's initials   witness's initials   witness's initials   testator's initials
WF-2

Any specific bequest made in this will to two or more beneficiaries shall be shared equally among them, unless unequal shares are specifically indicated.

If I name two or more primary beneficiaries to receive a specific gift of property and any of them do not survive me by 45 days, all surviving primary beneficiaries shall equally divide the deceased beneficiary's share. If I name two or more alternate beneficiaries to receive a specific gift of property and any of them do not survive me by 45 days, all surviving alternate beneficiaries shall equally divide the deceased alternate beneficiary's share.

5. **Residuary Estate.** I give my residuary estate, that is, the rest of my property not otherwise specifically and validly disposed of by this will or in any other manner, to _____ _____ or, if such residuary beneficiary(ies) do(es) not survive me by 45 days, to _____ _____ .

Any residuary bequest made in this will to two or more residuary beneficiaries shall be shared equally among them, unless unequal shares are specifically indicated.

If I name two or more residuary beneficiaries and any of them do not survive me by 45 days, all surviving residuary beneficiaries shall equally divide the deceased residuary beneficiary's share. If I name two or more alternate residuary beneficiaries to receive a specific gift of property and any of them do not survive me by 45 days, all surviving alternate residuary beneficiaries shall equally divide the deceased alternate residuary beneficiary's share.

6. **Executor.** I name _____ as executor, to serve without bond.

If that executor does not qualify or ceases to serve, I name_____ _____ as executor, also to serve without bond.

I direct that my executor take all actions legally permissible to probate this will, including filing a petition in the appropriate court for the independent administration of my estate.

I grant to my executor the following powers, to be exercised as the executor deems to be in the best interests of my estate:

(1) To retain property, without liability for loss or depreciation resulting from such retention.

(2) To sell, lease or exchange property and to receive or administer the proceeds as a part of my estate.

(3) To vote stock, convert bonds, notes, stocks or other securities belonging to my estate into other securities, and to exercise all other rights and privileges of a person owning similar property.

(4) To deal with and settle claims in favor of or against my estate.

(5) To continue, maintain, operate or participate in any business which is a part of my estate, and to incorporate, dissolve or otherwise change the form of organization of the business.

(6) To pay all debts and taxes that may be assessed against my estate, as provided under state law.

(7) To do all other acts, which in the executor's judgment may be necessary or appropriate for the proper and advantageous management, investment and distribution of my estate.

Page ___ of ___

WF-2

_____ _____ _____   _____
witness's initials   witness's initials   witness's initials   testator's initials

These powers, authority and discretion are in addition to the powers, authority and discretion vested in an executor by operation of law, and may be exercised as often as deemed necessary, without approval by any court in any jurisdiction.

I subscribe my name to this will this _____ day of _____ , 19 _____ , at _____ , State of _____ , and declare it is my last will, that I sign it willingly, that I execute it as my free and voluntary act for the purposes expressed, and that I am of the age of majority or otherwise legally empowered to make a will and under no constraint or undue influence.

_____
signature

WITNESSES

On this _____ day of _____ ,19 _____ , the testator, _____ , declared to us, the undersigned, that this instrument was his or her will and requested us to act as witnesses to it. The testator signed this will in our presence, all of us being present at the same time. We now, at the testator's request, in the testator's presence, and in the presence of each other, subscribe our names as witnesses and each declare that we are of sound mind and of proper age to witness a will. We further declare that we understand this to be the testator's will, and that to the best of our knowledge the testator is of the age of majority, or is otherwise legally empowered to make a will, and appears to be of sound mind and under no constraint or undue influence.

We declare under penalty of perjury that the foregoing is true and correct, this _____ day of _____ , 19 ____ , at _____ , State of _____ .

_____   _____
witness' signature   typed or printed name

residing at _____ , _____ ,
                        street address   city
_____ , _____ .
                        county   state

_____   _____
witness' signature   typed or printed name

residing at _____ , _____ ,
                        street address   city
_____ , _____ .
                        county   state

_____   _____
witness' signature   typed or printed name

residing at _____ , _____ ,
                        street address   city
_____ , _____ .
                        county   state

Will
of

_____

I, _____ ,

a resident of _____ , State of _____ ,

declare that this is my will.

    1. **Revocation.** I revoke all wills that I have previously made.

    2. **Marital Status.** I am not married.

    3. **Children.** I have the following children:

      Name _____ Date of Birth _____

    4. **Specific Bequests.** I make the following specific bequests of property:

    I give _____

_____

_____

to _____

or, if such beneficiary(ies) do(es) not survive me by 45 days, to _____

_____ .

    I give _____

_____

_____

to _____

or, if such beneficiary(ies) do(es) not survive me by 45 days, to _____

_____ .

    I give _____

_____

_____

to _____

or, if such beneficiary(ies) do(es) not survive me by 45 days, to _____

_____ .

I give _____

_____

_____

to _____
or, if such beneficiary(ies) do(es) not survive me by 45 days, to _____

_____ .

    I give _____

_____

_____

to _____
or, if such beneficiary(ies) do(es) not survive me by 45 days, to _____

_____ .

    I give _____

_____

_____

to _____
or, if such beneficiary(ies) do(es) not survive me by 45 days, to _____

_____ .

    I give _____

_____

_____

to _____
or, if such beneficiary(ies) do(es) not survive me by 45 days, to _____

_____ .

    I give _____

_____

_____

to _____
or, if such beneficiary(ies) do(es) not survive me by 45 days, to _____

_____ .

    I give _____

_____

_____

to _____
or, if such beneficiary(ies) do(es) not survive me by 45 days, to _____

_____ .

Any specific bequest made in this will to two or more beneficiaries shall be shared equally among them, unless unequal shares are specifically indicated.

If I name two or more primary beneficiaries to receive a specific gift of property and any of them do not survive me by 45 days, all surviving primary beneficiaries shall equally divide the deceased beneficiary's share. If I name two or more alternate beneficiaries to receive a specific gift of property and any of them do not survive me by 45 days, all surviving alternate beneficiaries shall equally divide the deceased alternate beneficiary's share.

5. **Residuary Estate.** I give my residuary estate, that is, the rest of my property not otherwise specifically and validly disposed of by this will or in any other manner, to _____ _____ or, if such residuary beneficiary(ies) do(es) not survive me by 45 days, to _____ _____ .

Any residuary bequest made in this will to two or more residuary beneficiaries shall be shared equally among them, unless unequal shares are specifically indicated.

If I name two or more residuary beneficiaries and any of them do not survive me by 45 days, all surviving residuary beneficiaries shall equally divide the deceased residuary beneficiary's share. If I name two or more alternate residuary beneficiaries to receive a specific gift of property and any of them do not survive me by 45 days, all surviving alternate residuary beneficiaries shall equally divide the deceased alternate residuary beneficiary's share.

6. **Executor.** I name _____ as executor, to serve without bond.

If that executor does not qualify or ceases to serve, I name_____ _____ as executor, also to serve without bond.

I direct that my executor take all actions legally permissible to probate this will, including filing a petition in the appropriate court for the independent administration of my estate.

I grant to my executor the following powers, to be exercised as the executor deems to be in the best interests of my estate:

(1) To retain property, without liability for loss or depreciation resulting from such retention.

(2) To sell, lease or exchange property and to receive or administer the proceeds as a part of my estate.

(3) To vote stock, convert bonds, notes, stocks or other securities belonging to my estate into other securities, and to exercise all other rights and privileges of a person owning similar property.

(4) To deal with and settle claims in favor of or against my estate.

(5) To continue, maintain, operate or participate in any business which is a part of my estate, and to incorporate, dissolve or otherwise change the form of organization of the business.

(6) To pay all debts and taxes that may be assessed against my estate, as provided under state law.

(7) To do all other acts, which in the executor's judgment may be necessary or appropriate for the proper and advantageous management, investment and distribution of my estate.

Page ___ of ___

WF-3

_____ witness's initials _____ witness's initials _____ witness's initials _____ testator's initials

These powers, authority and discretion are in addition to the powers, authority and discretion vested in an executor by operation of law, and may be exercised as often as deemed necessary, without approval by any court in any jurisdiction.

7. **Personal Guardian.** If at my death any of my children are minors and a personal guardian is needed, I name

_____

as the personal guardian, to serve without bond.

If this person is unable or unwilling to serve as personal guardian, I name _____

_____ as personal guardian, also to serve without bond.

8. **Property Guardian.** If any of my children are minors and a property guardian is needed, I name

_____ as the property guardian, to serve without bond.

If this person is unable or unwilling to serve as property guardian, I name _____

_____ as property guardian, also to serve without bond.

9. **Children's Trust.** All property I give in this will to any of the children listed in Section A, below, shall be held for each of them in a separate trust, administered according to the following terms:

A. Trust Beneficiaries and Age Limits

Each trust shall end when the following beneficiaries become 35, except as otherwise specified in this section.

Trust Beneficiary _____ Trust Shall End At Age _____

B. Trustees

I name _____ as trustee, to serve without bond.

If this person is unable or unwilling to serve as trustee, I name _____

_____ as trustee, also to serve without bond.

C. Beneficiary Provisions

(1) The trustee may distribute for the benefit of the beneficiary as much of the net income or principal of the trust as the trustee deems necessary for the beneficiary's health, support, maintenance and education. In deciding whether to make a distribution to the beneficiary, the trustee may take into account the beneficiary's other income, resources and sources of support.

(2) Any trust income that is not distributed to a beneficiary by the trustee shall be accumulated and added to the principal of the trust administered for that beneficiary.

D. Termination of Trust

The trust shall terminate when any of the following occurs:

(1) The beneficiary becomes the age specified in Paragraph A of this trust;

(2) The beneficiary dies before becoming the age specified in Paragraph A of this trust;

(3) The trust property is used up through distributions allowed under these provisions.

If the trust terminates because the beneficiary reaches the specified age, the remaining principal and accumulated net income of the trust shall pass to the beneficiary. If the trust terminates because the beneficiary dies, the remaining principal and accumulated net income of the trust shall pass to the trust beneficiary's heirs.

E. Powers of Trustee

In addition to other powers granted to the trustee in this will, the trustee shall have:

(1) All the powers generally conferred on trustees by the laws of the state having jurisdiction over this trust;

(2) With respect to property in the trust, the powers conferred by this will on the executor; and

(3) The authority to hire and pay from the trust assets the reasonable fees of investment advisors, accountants, tax advisors, agents, attorneys and other assistants to administer the trust and manage any trust asset and for any litigation affecting the trust.

F. Trust Administration Provisions

(1) This trust shall be administered independent of court supervision to the maximum extent possible under the laws of the state having jurisdiction over this trust.

(2) The interests of trust beneficiaries shall not be transferable by voluntary or involuntary assignment or by operation of law and shall be free from the claims of creditors and from attachment, execution, bankruptcy or other legal process to the fullest extent permissible by law.

(3) Any trustee serving shall be entitled to reasonable compensation out of the trust assets for ordinary and extraordinary services, and for all services in connection with the complete or partial termination of any trust created by this will.

(4) The invalidity of any provision of this trust instrument shall not affect the validity of the remaining provisions.

I subscribe my name to this will this _____ day of _____ , 19 _____ , at
_____ , State of _____ ,
and declare it is my last will, that I sign it willingly, that I execute it as my free and voluntary act for the purposes expressed, and that I am of the age of majority or otherwise legally empowered to make a will and under no constraint or undue influence.

_____
signature

WITNESSES

On this _____ day of _____ ,19 _____ , the testator,
_____ , declared to us, the undersigned, that this instrument was his or her will and requested us to act as witnesses to it. The testator signed this will in our presence, all of us being present at the same time. We now, at the testator's request, in the testator's presence,

_____   _____   _____   _____
witness's initials   witness's initials   witness's initials   testator's initials

and in the presence of each other, subscribe our names as witnesses and each declare that we are of sound mind and of proper age to witness a will. We further declare that we understand this to be the testator's will, and that to the best of our knowledge the testator is of the age of majority, or is otherwise legally empowered to make a will, and appears to be of sound mind and under no constraint or undue influence.

    We declare under penalty of perjury that the foregoing is true and correct, this _____ day of _____ , 19 _____ , at _____ , State of _____ .

_____
                         witness' signature   typed or printed name

residing at _____ , _____ ,
                            street address   city

_____ , _____ .
                        county   state

_____
                         witness' signature   typed or printed name

residing at _____ , _____ ,
                            street address   city

_____ , _____ .
                        county   state

_____
                         witness' signature   typed or printed name

residing at _____ , _____ ,
                            street address   city

_____ , _____ .
                        county   state

       _____   _____   _____   _____
       witness's initials   witness's initials   witness's initials   testator's initials

Will

of

_____

I, _____ ,

a resident of _____ , State of _____ ,

declare that this is my will.

1. **Revocation.** I revoke all wills that I have previously made.

2. **Marital Status.** I am married to _____ .

3. **Children.** I do not have any children.

4. **Specific Bequests.** I make the following specific bequests of property:

I give _____

_____

_____

to _____

or, if such beneficiary(ies) do(es) not survive me by 45 days, to _____

_____ .

I give _____

_____

_____

to _____

or, if such beneficiary(ies) do(es) not survive me by 45 days, to _____

_____ .

I give _____

_____

_____

to _____

or, if such beneficiary(ies) do(es) not survive me by 45 days, to _____

_____ .

I give _____

_____

_____

to _____

or, if such beneficiary(ies) do(es) not survive me by 45 days, to _____

_____ .

_____   _____   _____   _____
witness's initials   witness's initials   witness's initials   testator's initials

WF-4

I give _____

_____

_____

to _____

or, if such beneficiary(ies) do(es) not survive me by 45 days, to _____

_____ .

I give _____

_____

_____

to _____

or, if such beneficiary(ies) do(es) not survive me by 45 days, to _____

_____ .

I give _____

_____

_____

to _____

or, if such beneficiary(ies) do(es) not survive me by 45 days, to _____

_____ .

I give _____

_____

_____

to _____

or, if such beneficiary(ies) do(es) not survive me by 45 days, to _____

_____ .

I give _____

_____

_____

to _____

or, if such beneficiary(ies) do(es) not survive me by 45 days, to _____

_____ .

I give _____

_____

_____

to _____

or, if such beneficiary(ies) do(es) not survive me by 45 days, to _____

_____ .

_____   _____   _____   _____
witness's initials   witness's initials   witness's initials   testator's initials

WF-4

Any specific bequest made in this will to two or more beneficiaries shall be shared equally among them, unless unequal shares are specifically indicated.

If I name two or more primary beneficiaries to receive a specific gift of property and any of them do not survive me by 45 days, all surviving primary beneficiaries shall equally divide the deceased beneficiary's share. If I name two or more alternate beneficiaries to receive a specific gift of property and any of them do not survive me by 45 days, all surviving alternate beneficiaries shall equally divide the deceased alternate beneficiary's share.

5. **Residuary Estate.** I give my residuary estate, that is, the rest of my property not otherwise specifically and validly disposed of by this will or in any other manner, to _____ _____ or, if such residuary beneficiary(ies) do(es) not survive me by 45 days, to _____ _____ .

Any residuary bequest made in this will to two or more residuary beneficiaries shall be shared equally among them, unless unequal shares are specifically indicated.

If I name two or more residuary beneficiaries and any of them do not survive me by 45 days, all surviving residuary beneficiaries shall equally divide the deceased residuary beneficiary's share. If I name two or more alternate residuary beneficiaries to receive a specific gift of property and any of them do not survive me by 45 days, all surviving alternate residuary beneficiaries shall equally divide the deceased alternate residuary beneficiary's share.

6. **Executor.** I name _____ as executor, to serve without bond.

If that executor does not qualify or ceases to serve, I name_____ _____ as executor, also to serve without bond.

I direct that my executor take all actions legally permissible to probate this will, including filing a petition in the appropriate court for the independent administration of my estate.

I grant to my executor the following powers, to be exercised as the executor deems to be in the best interests of my estate:

(1) To retain property, without liability for loss or depreciation resulting from such retention.

(2) To sell, lease or exchange property and to receive or administer the proceeds as a part of my estate.

(3) To vote stock, convert bonds, notes, stocks or other securities belonging to my estate into other securities, and to exercise all other rights and privileges of a person owning similar property.

(4) To deal with and settle claims in favor of or against my estate.

(5) To continue, maintain, operate or participate in any business which is a part of my estate, and to incorporate, dissolve or otherwise change the form of organization of the business.

(6) To pay all debts and taxes that may be assessed against my estate, as provided under state law.

(7) To do all other acts, which in the executor's judgment may be necessary or appropriate for the proper and advantageous management, investment and distribution of my estate.

Page ___ of ___

WF-4

_____ _____ _____ _____
witness's initials witness's initials witness's initials testator's initials

These powers, authority and discretion are in addition to the powers, authority and discretion vested in an executor by operation of law, and may be exercised as often as deemed necessary, without approval by any court in any jurisdiction.

I subscribe my name to this will this _____ day of _____, 19 _____ , at _____ , State of _____ , and declare it is my last will, that I sign it willingly, that I execute it as my free and voluntary act for the purposes expressed, and that I am of the age of majority or otherwise legally empowered to make a will and under no constraint or undue influence.

_____
signature

WITNESSES

On this _____ day of_____ ,19 _____ , the testator, _____ , declared to us, the undersigned, that this instrument was his or her will and requested us to act as witnesses to it. The testator signed this will in our presence, all of us being present at the same time. We now, at the testator's request, in the testator's presence, and in the presence of each other, subscribe our names as witnesses and each declare that we are of sound mind and of proper age to witness a will. We further declare that we understand this to be the testator's will, and that to the best of our knowledge the testator is of the age of majority, or is otherwise legally empowered to make a will, and appears to be of sound mind and under no constraint or undue influence.

We declare under penalty of perjury that the foregoing is true and correct, this _____ day of_____ , 19 _____ , at _____ , State of _____ .

_____ _____
witness' signature   typed or printed name

residing at _____ , _____ ,
                                   street address   city

_____ , _____ .
                                   county   state

_____ _____
witness' signature   typed or printed name

residing at _____ , _____ ,
                                   street address   city

_____ , _____ .
                                   county   state

_____ _____
witness' signature   typed or printed name

residing at _____ , _____ ,
                                   street address   city

_____ , _____ .
                                   county   state

_____   _____   _____   _____
witness's initials   witness's initials   witness's initials   testator's initials

Will

of

_____

I, _____ ,

a resident of _____ , State of _____ ,

declare that this is my will.

1. **Revocation.** I revoke all wills that I have previously made.

2. **Marital Status.** I am married to _____ .

3. **Children.** I have the following children:

Name   Date of Birth _____

4. **Specific Bequests.** I make the following specific bequests of property:

I give _____

_____

_____

to _____

or, if such beneficiary(ies) do(es) not survive me by 45 days, to _____

_____ .

I give _____

_____

_____

to _____

or, if such beneficiary(ies) do(es) not survive me by 45 days, to _____

_____ .

I give _____

_____

_____

to _____

or, if such beneficiary(ies) do(es) not survive me by 45 days, to _____

_____ .

I give _____

_____

_____

to _____

or, if such beneficiary(ies) do(es) not survive me by 45 days, to _____

_____ .

I give _____

_____

_____

to _____

or, if such beneficiary(ies) do(es) not survive me by 45 days, to _____

_____ .

I give _____

_____

_____

to _____

or, if such beneficiary(ies) do(es) not survive me by 45 days, to _____

_____ .

I give _____

_____

_____

to _____

or, if such beneficiary(ies) do(es) not survive me by 45 days, to _____

_____ .

I give _____

_____

_____

to _____

or, if such beneficiary(ies) do(es) not survive me by 45 days, to _____

_____ .

I give _____

_____

_____

to _____

or, if such beneficiary(ies) do(es) not survive me by 45 days, to _____

_____ .

_____   _____   _____   _____
witness's initials   witness's initials   witness's initials   testator's initials

Any specific bequest made in this will to two or more beneficiaries shall be shared equally among them, unless unequal shares are specifically indicated.

If I name two or more primary beneficiaries to receive a specific gift of property and any of them do not survive me by 45 days, all surviving primary beneficiaries shall equally divide the deceased beneficiary's share. If I name two or more alternate beneficiaries to receive a specific gift of property and any of them do not survive me by 45 days, all surviving alternate beneficiaries shall equally divide the deceased alternate beneficiary's share.

5. **Residuary Estate.** I give my residuary estate, that is, the rest of my property not otherwise specifically and validly disposed of by this will or in any other manner, to _____ _____ or, if such residuary beneficiary(ies) do(es) not survive me by 45 days, to _____ _____ .

Any residuary bequest made in this will to two or more residuary beneficiaries shall be shared equally among them, unless unequal shares are specifically indicated.

If I name two or more residuary beneficiaries and any of them do not survive me by 45 days, all surviving residuary beneficiaries shall equally divide the deceased residuary beneficiary's share. If I name two or more alternate residuary beneficiaries to receive a specific gift of property and any of them do not survive me by 45 days, all surviving alternate residuary beneficiaries shall equally divide the deceased alternate residuary beneficiary's share.

6. **Executor.** I name _____ as executor, to serve without bond.

If that executor does not qualify or ceases to serve, I name_____ _____ as executor, also to serve without bond.

I direct that my executor take all actions legally permissible to probate this will, including filing a petition in the appropriate court for the independent administration of my estate.

I grant to my executor the following powers, to be exercised as the executor deems to be in the best interests of my estate:

(1) To retain property, without liability for loss or depreciation resulting from such retention.

(2) To sell, lease or exchange property and to receive or administer the proceeds as a part of my estate.

(3) To vote stock, convert bonds, notes, stocks or other securities belonging to my estate into other securities, and to exercise all other rights and privileges of a person owning similar property.

(4) To deal with and settle claims in favor of or against my estate.

(5) To continue, maintain, operate or participate in any business which is a part of my estate, and to incorporate, dissolve or otherwise change the form of organization of the business.

(6) To pay all debts and taxes that may be assessed against my estate, as provided under state law.

(7) To do all other acts, which in the executor's judgment may be necessary or appropriate for the proper and advantageous management, investment and distribution of my estate.

These powers, authority and discretion are in addition to the powers, authority and discretion vested in an executor by operation of law, and may be exercised as often as deemed necessary, without approval by any court in any jurisdiction.

I subscribe my name to this will this _____ day of _____ , 19 _____ , at _____ , State of _____ , and declare it is my last will, that I sign it willingly, that I execute it as my free and voluntary act for the purposes expressed, and that I am of the age of majority or otherwise legally empowered to make a will and under no constraint or undue influence.

_____
signature

WITNESSES

On this _____ day of_____ ,19 _____ , the testator, _____ , declared to us, the undersigned, that this instrument was his or her will and requested us to act as witnesses to it. The testator signed this will in our presence, all of us being present at the same time. We now, at the testator's request, in the testator's presence, and in the presence of each other, subscribe our names as witnesses and each declare that we are of sound mind and of proper age to witness a will. We further declare that we understand this to be the testator's will, and that to the best of our knowledge the testator is of the age of majority, or is otherwise legally empowered to make a will, and appears to be of sound mind and under no constraint or undue influence.

We declare under penalty of perjury that the foregoing is true and correct, this _____ day of _____ , 19 _____ , at _____ , State of _____ .

_____   _____
witness' signature   typed or printed name

residing at _____ , _____ ,
street address   city

_____ , _____ .
county   state

_____   _____
witness' signature   typed or printed name

residing at _____ , _____ ,
street address   city

_____ , _____ .
county   state

_____   _____
witness' signature   typed or printed name

residing at _____ , _____ ,
street address   city

_____ , _____ .
county   state

Page ___ of ___   _____   _____   _____   _____
witness's initials   witness's initials   witness's initials   testator's initials
WF-5

Will

of

_____

I, _____ ,

a resident of _____ , State of _____ ,

declare that this is my will.

    1. **Revocation.** I revoke all wills that I have previously made.

    2. **Marital Status.** I am married to _____ .

    3. **Children.** I have the following children:

      Name _____ Date of Birth _____

    4. **Specific Bequests.** I make the following specific bequests of property:

      I give _____

_____

_____

to _____

or, if such beneficiary(ies) do(es) not survive me by 45 days, to _____

_____ .

      I give _____

_____

_____

to _____

or, if such beneficiary(ies) do(es) not survive me by 45 days, to _____

_____ .

      I give _____

_____

_____

to _____

or, if such beneficiary(ies) do(es) not survive me by 45 days, to _____

_____ .

_____ _____ _____   _____
witness's initials   witness's initials   witness's initials   testator's initials

WF-6

I give _____

_____

_____

to _____
or, if such beneficiary(ies) do(es) not survive me by 45 days, to _____

_____.

    I give _____

_____

_____

to _____
or, if such beneficiary(ies) do(es) not survive me by 45 days, to _____

_____.

    I give _____

_____

_____

to _____
or, if such beneficiary(ies) do(es) not survive me by 45 days, to _____

_____.

    I give _____

_____

_____

to _____
or, if such beneficiary(ies) do(es) not survive me by 45 days, to _____

_____.

    I give _____

_____

_____

to _____
or, if such beneficiary(ies) do(es) not survive me by 45 days, to _____

_____.

    I give _____

_____

_____

to _____
or, if such beneficiary(ies) do(es) not survive me by 45 days, to _____

_____.

_____   _____   _____   _____
witness's initials   witness's initials   witness's initials   testator's initials

WF-6

Any specific bequest made in this will to two or more beneficiaries shall be shared equally among them, unless unequal shares are specifically indicated.

If I name two or more primary beneficiaries to receive a specific gift of property and any of them do not survive me by 45 days, all surviving primary beneficiaries shall equally divide the deceased beneficiary's share. If I name two or more alternate beneficiaries to receive a specific gift of property and any of them do not survive me by 45 days, all surviving alternate beneficiaries shall equally divide the deceased alternate beneficiary's share.

5. **Residuary Estate.** I give my residuary estate, that is, the rest of my property not otherwise specifically and validly disposed of by this will or in any other manner, to _____ _____ or, if such residuary beneficiary(ies) do(es) not survive me by 45 days, to _____ _____ .

Any residuary bequest made in this will to two or more residuary beneficiaries shall be shared equally among them, unless unequal shares are specifically indicated.

If I name two or more residuary beneficiaries and any of them do not survive me by 45 days, all surviving residuary beneficiaries shall equally divide the deceased residuary beneficiary's share. If I name two or more alternate residuary beneficiaries to receive a specific gift of property and any of them do not survive me by 45 days, all surviving alternate residuary beneficiaries shall equally divide the deceased alternate residuary beneficiary's share.

6. **Executor.** I name _____ as executor, to serve without bond.

If that executor does not qualify or ceases to serve, I name_____ _____ as executor, also to serve without bond.

I direct that my executor take all actions legally permissible to probate this will, including filing a petition in the appropriate court for the independent administration of my estate.

I grant to my executor the following powers, to be exercised as the executor deems to be in the best interests of my estate:

(1) To retain property, without liability for loss or depreciation resulting from such retention.

(2) To sell, lease or exchange property and to receive or administer the proceeds as a part of my estate.

(3) To vote stock, convert bonds, notes, stocks or other securities belonging to my estate into other securities, and to exercise all other rights and privileges of a person owning similar property.

(4) To deal with and settle claims in favor of or against my estate.

(5) To continue, maintain, operate or participate in any business which is a part of my estate, and to incorporate, dissolve or otherwise change the form of organization of the business.

(6) To pay all debts and taxes that may be assessed against my estate, as provided under state law.

(7) To do all other acts, which in the executor's judgment may be necessary or appropriate for the proper and advantageous management, investment and distribution of my estate.

Page ___ of ___

_____ _____ _____ _____
witness's initials witness's initials witness's initials testator's initials

WF-6

These powers, authority and discretion are in addition to the powers, authority and discretion vested in an executor by operation of law, and may be exercised as often as deemed necessary, without approval by any court in any jurisdiction.

7. **Personal Guardian.** If at my death any of my children are minors and a personal guardian is needed, I name _____

as the personal guardian, to serve without bond.

If this person is unable or unwilling to serve as personal guardian, I name _____

_____ as personal guardian, also to serve without bond.

8. **Property Guardian.** If any of my children are minors and a property guardian is needed, I name _____ as the property guardian, to serve without bond.

If this person is unable or unwilling to serve as property guardian, I name _____

_____ as property guardian, also to serve without bond.

9. **Children's Trust.** All property I give in this will to any of the children listed in Section A, below, shall be held for each of them in a separate trust, administered according to the following terms:

A. Trust Beneficiaries and Age Limits

Each trust shall end when the following beneficiaries become 35, except as otherwise specified in this section.

Trust Beneficiary	Trust Shall End At Age

B. Trustees

I name _____ as trustee, to serve without bond.

If this person is unable or unwilling to serve as trustee, I name _____

_____ as trustee, also to serve without bond.

C. Beneficiary Provisions

(1) The trustee may distribute for the benefit of the beneficiary as much of the net income or principal of the trust as the trustee deems necessary for the beneficiary's health, support, maintenance and education. In deciding whether to make a distribution to the beneficiary, the trustee may take into account the beneficiary's other income, resources and sources of support.

(2) Any trust income that is not distributed to a beneficiary by the trustee shall be accumulated and added to the principal of the trust administered for that beneficiary.

D. Termination of Trust

The trust shall terminate when any of the following occurs:

Page ___ of ___

WF-6

_____ witness's initials   _____ witness's initials   _____ witness's initials   _____ testator's initials

(1) The beneficiary becomes the age specified in Paragraph A of this trust;

(2) The beneficiary dies before becoming the age specified in Paragraph A of this trust;

(3) The trust property is used up through distributions allowed under these provisions.

If the trust terminates because the beneficiary reaches the specified age, the remaining principal and accumulated net income of the trust shall pass to the beneficiary. If the trust terminates because the beneficiary dies, the remaining principal and accumulated net income of the trust shall pass to the trust beneficiary's heirs.

E. Powers of Trustee

In addition to other powers granted to the trustee in this will, the trustee shall have:

(1) All the powers generally conferred on trustees by the laws of the state having jurisdiction over this trust;

(2) With respect to property in the trust, the powers conferred by this will on the executor; and

(3) The authority to hire and pay from the trust assets the reasonable fees of investment advisors, accountants, tax advisors, agents, attorneys and other assistants to administer the trust and manage any trust asset and for any litigation affecting the trust.

F. Trust Administration Provisions

(1) This trust shall be administered independent of court supervision to the maximum extent possible under the laws of the state having jurisdiction over this trust.

(2) The interests of trust beneficiaries shall not be transferable by voluntary or involuntary assignment or by operation of law and shall be free from the claims of creditors and from attachment, execution, bankruptcy or other legal process to the fullest extent permissible by law.

(3) Any trustee serving shall be entitled to reasonable compensation out of the trust assets for ordinary and extraordinary services, and for all services in connection with the complete or partial termination of any trust created by this will.

(4) The invalidity of any provision of this trust instrument shall not affect the validity of the remaining provisions.

I subscribe my name to this will this _____ day of _____, 19 _____ , at
_____ , State of _____ ,
and declare it is my last will, that I sign it willingly, that I execute it as my free and voluntary act for the purposes expressed, and that I am of the age of majority or otherwise legally empowered to make a will and under no constraint or undue influence.

_____
signature

WITNESSES

On this _____ day of _____ ,19 _____ , the testator,
_____ , declared to us, the undersigned, that this instrument was his or her will and requested us to act as witnesses to it. The testator signed this will in our

presence, all of us being present at the same time. We now, at the testator's request, in the testator's presence, and in the presence of each other, subscribe our names as witnesses and each declare that we are of sound mind and of proper age to witness a will. We further declare that we understand this to be the testator's will, and that to the best of our knowledge the testator is of the age of majority, or is otherwise legally empowered to make a will, and appears to be of sound mind and under no constraint or undue influence.

    We declare under penalty of perjury that the foregoing is true and correct, this _____ day of _____ , 19____ , at _____ ,

State of _____ .

_____   _____
               witness' signature   typed or printed name

residing at _____ , _____ ,
                      street address   city

_____ , _____ .
                      county   state

_____   _____
               witness' signature   typed or printed name

residing at _____ , _____ ,
                      street address   city

_____ , _____ .
                      county   state

_____   _____
               witness' signature   typed or printed name

residing at _____ , _____ ,
                      street address   city

_____ , _____ .
                      county   state

Page ___ of ___   _____   _____   _____   _____
                  witness's initials   witness's initials   witness's initials   testator's initials

WF-6

I give _____

_____

_____

to _____

or, if such beneficiary(ies) do(es) not survive me by 45 days, to _____

_____ .

I give _____

_____

_____

to _____

or, if such beneficiary(ies) do(es) not survive me by 45 days, to _____

_____ .

I give _____

_____

_____

to _____

or, if such beneficiary(ies) do(es) not survive me by 45 days, to _____

_____ .

I give _____

_____

_____

to _____

or, if such beneficiary(ies) do(es) not survive me by 45 days, to _____

_____ .

I give _____

_____

_____

to _____

or, if such beneficiary(ies) do(es) not survive me by 45 days, to _____

_____ .

| _____ | _____ | _____ | _____ |
| witness's initials | witness's initials | witness's initials | testator's initials |

WF-SB

I give _____

_____

_____

to _____

or, if such beneficiary(ies) do(es) not survive me by 45 days, to _____

_____ .

I give _____

_____

_____

to _____

or, if such beneficiary(ies) do(es) not survive me by 45 days, to _____

_____ .

I give _____

_____

_____

to _____

or, if such beneficiary(ies) do(es) not survive me by 45 days, to _____

_____ .

I give _____

_____

_____

to _____

or, if such beneficiary(ies) do(es) not survive me by 45 days, to _____

_____ .

I give _____

_____

_____

to _____

or, if such beneficiary(ies) do(es) not survive me by 45 days, to _____

_____ .

I give _____

_____

_____

to _____

or, if such beneficiary(ies) do(es) not survive me by 45 days, to _____

_____ .

_____   _____   _____   _____
witness's initials   witness's initials   witness's initials   testator's initials

WF-SB

SPECIFIC BEQUESTS WORKSHEET

Describe property you wish to leave in specific bequests:	Select beneficiaries for specific bequests:	
	Primary beneficiary(ies) (1st choice)	Alternate beneficiary(ies) (2nd choice)

SBW

SPECIFIC BEQUESTS WORKSHEET

Describe property you wish to leave in specific bequests:	Select beneficiaries for specific bequests:	
	Primary beneficiary(ies) (1st choice)	Alternate beneficiary(ies) (2nd choice)

AFFIDAVIT

We, _____ ,

_____ ,

_____ and

_____ , the

testator and the witnesses, whose names are signed to the attached instrument in those capacities, personally appearing before the undersigned authority and being first duly sworn, declare to the undersigned authority under penalty of perjury that:

1) the testator declared, signed and executed the instrument as his or her last will;

2) he or she signed it willingly or directed another to sign for him or her;

3) he or she executed it as his or her free and voluntary act for the purposes therein expressed; and

4) each of the witnesses, at the request of the testator, in his or her hearing and presence, and in the presence of each other, signed the will as witness and that to the best of his or her knowledge the testator was at that time of full legal age, of sound mind and under no constraint or undue influence.

Testator: _____

Witness: _____

Address: _____

Witness: _____

Address: _____

Witness: _____

Address: _____

Subscribed, sworn and acknowledged before me, _____ ,

a notary public, by _____ ,

the testator, and by _____ ,

_____ ,

and _____ ,

the witnesses, this _____ day of _____ , 19 _____ .

[NOTARY SEAL]   _____

                                              Signature of notary public

                                              My commission expires:_____

AFFIDAVIT

STATE OF _____

COUNTY OF _____

I, the undersigned, an officer authorized to administer oaths, certify that _____

_____ , the testator, and

_____ ,

_____ and

_____ , the witnesses,

whose names are signed to the attached or foregoing instrument and whose signatures appear below, having

appeared together before me and having been first duly sworn, each then declared to me that:

1) the attached or foregoing instrument is the last will of the testator;

2) the testator willingly and voluntarily declared, signed and executed the will in the presence of the

   witnesses;

3) the witnesses signed the will upon request by the testator, in the presence and hearing of the testator,

   and in the presence of each other;

4) to the best knowledge of each witness the testator was, at that time of the signing, of the age of majority

   (or otherwise legally competent to make a will), of sound mind, and under no constraint or undue

   influence; and

5) each witness was and is competent, and of the proper age to witness a will.

Testator: _____

Witness: _____

Address: _____

Witness: _____

Address: _____

Witness: _____

Address: _____

Subscribed, sworn and acknowledged before me, _____ ,

a notary public, by _____ ,

the testator, and by _____ ,

_____ ,

and _____ ,

the witnesses, this _____ day of _____ , 19 _____ .

SIGNED: _____

_____
OFFICIAL CAPACITY OF OFFICER

Aff-2

AFFIDAVIT

THE STATE OF TEXAS

COUNTY OF _____

    Before me, the undersigned authority, on this day personally appeared _____ _____ , _____ _____ , and _____ _____ , known to me to be the testator and the witnesses, respectively, whose names are subscribed to the annexed or foregoing instrument in their respective capacities, and, all of said persons being by me duly sworn, the said _____ _____ , testator, declared to me and to the said witnesses in my presence that said instrument is his or her last will and testament, and that he or she had willingly made and executed it as his or her free act and deed; and the said witnesses, each on his or her oath stated to me, in the presence and hearing of the said testator, that the said testator had declared to them that said instrument is his or her last will and testament, and that he or she executed same as such and wanted each of them to sign it as a witness; and upon their oaths each witness stated further that they did sign the same as witnesses in the presence of the said testator and at his or her request; that he or she was at the time eighteen years of age or over (or being under such age, was or had been lawfully married, or was then a member of the armed forces of the United States or an auxiliary thereof or of the Maritime Service) and was of sound mind; and that each of said witnesses was then at least fourteen years of age.

Testator: _____

Witness: _____

Witness: _____

    Subscribed and sworn to before me by the said _____ _____ , testator, and by the said _____ , and _____ , witnesses, this _____ day of _____ ,19 _____ .

SIGNED: _____

_____
(Official Capacity of Officer)

CATALOG

...more from Nolo Press

		PRICE	CODE

BUSINESS

	The California Nonprofit Corporation Handbook	$29.95	NON
	The California Professional Corporation Handbook	$34.95	PROF
	The Employer's Legal Handbook	$29.95	EMPL
	Form Your Own Limited Liability Company	$34.95	LIAB
🖬	Hiring Independent Contractors: The Employer's Legal Guide, (Book w/Disk—PC)	$29.95	HICI
🖬	How to Form a CA Nonprofit Corp.—w/Corp. Records Binder & PC Disk	$49.95	CNP
🖬	How to Form a Nonprofit Corp., Book w/Disk (PC)—National Edition	$39.95	NNP
🖬	How to Form Your Own Calif. Corp.—w/Corp. Records Binder & Disk—PC	$39.95	CACI
	How to Form Your Own California Corporation	$29.95	CCOR
🖬	How to Form Your Own Florida Corporation, (Book w/Disk—PC)	$39.95	FLCO
🖬	How to Form Your Own New York Corporation, (Book w/Disk—PC)	$39.95	NYCO
🖬	How to Form Your Own Texas Corporation, (Book w/Disk—PC)	$39.95	TCOR
	How to Handle Your Workers' Compensation Claim (California Edition)	$29.95	WORK
	How to Market a Product for Under $500	$29.95	UN500
	How to Mediate Your Dispute	$18.95	MEDI
	How to Write a Business Plan	$21.95	SBS
	The Independent Paralegal's Handbook	$29.95	PARA
	Legal Guide for Starting & Running a Small Business, Vol. 1	$24.95	RUNS
🖬	Legal Guide for Starting & Running a Small Business, Vol. 2: Legal Forms	$29.95	RUNS2
	Marketing Without Advertising	$19.00	MWAD
🖬	The Partnership Book: How to Write a Partnership Agreement, (Book w/Disk—PC)	$34.95	PART
	Sexual Harassment on the Job	$18.95	HARS
	Starting and Running a Successful Newsletter or Magazine	$24.95	MAG
🖬	Taking Care of Your Corporation, Vol. 1, (Book w/Disk—PC)	$29.95	CORK
🖬	Taking Care of Your Corporation, Vol. 2, (Book w/Disk—PC)	$39.95	CORK2
	Tax Savvy for Small Business	$28.95	SAVVY
	Trademark: Legal Care for Your Business and Product Name	$29.95	TRD
	Wage Slave No More: The Independent Contractor's Legal Guide	$34.95	WAGE
	Your Rights in the Workplace	$19.95	YRW

CONSUMER

Fed Up With the Legal System: What's Wrong & How to Fix It	$9.95	LEG
How to Win Your Personal Injury Claim	$24.95	PICL
Nolo's Everyday Law Book	$21.95	EVL
Nolo's Pocket Guide to California Law	$11.95	CLAW
Trouble-Free Travel...And What to Do When Things Go Wrong	$14.95	TRAV

🖬 Book with disk

● Book with CD-ROM

	PRICE	CODE

ESTATE PLANNING & PROBATE

	PRICE	CODE
8 Ways to Avoid Probate (Quick & Legal Series)	$15.95	PRO8
How to Probate an Estate (California Edition)	$34.95	PAE
Make Your Own Living Trust	$21.95	LITR
Nolo's Will Book, (Book w/Disk—PC)	$29.95	SWIL
Plan Your Estate	$24.95	NEST
The Quick and Legal Will Book	$15.95	QUIC
Nolo's Law Form Kit: Wills	$14.95	KWL

FAMILY MATTERS

	PRICE	CODE
A Legal Guide for Lesbian and Gay Couples	$24.95	LG
California Marriage Law	$19.95	MARR
Child Custody: Building Parenting Agreements that Work	$24.95	CUST
Divorce & Money: How to Make the Best Financial Decisions During Divorce	$26.95	DIMO
Get A Life: You Don't Need a Million to Retire Well	$18.95	LIFE
The Guardianship Book (California Edition)	$24.95	GB
How to Adopt Your Stepchild in California	$22.95	ADOP
How to Do Your Own Divorce in California	$24.95	CDIV
How to Do Your Own Divorce in Texas	$19.95	TDIV
How to Raise or Lower Child Support in California	$18.95	CHLD
The Living Together Kit	$24.95	LTK
Nolo's Law Form Kit: Hiring Childcare & Household Help	$14.95	KCHLO
Nolo's Pocket Guide to Family Law	$14.95	FLD
Practical Divorce Solutions	$14.95	PDS
Smart Ways to Save Money During and After Divorce	$14.95	SAVMO

GOING TO COURT

	PRICE	CODE
Collect Your Court Judgment (California Edition)	$24.95	JUDG
How to Seal Your Juvenile & Criminal Records (California Edition)	$24.95	CRIM
How to Sue For Up to 25,000...and Win!	$29.95	MUNI
Everybody's Guide to Small Claims Court in California	$18.95	CSCC
Everybody's Guide to Small Claims Court (National Edition)	$18.95	NSCC
Fight Your Ticket ... and Win! (California Edition)	$19.95	FYT
How to Change Your Name (California Edition)	$24.95	NAME
Mad at Your Lawyer	$21.95	MAD
Represent Yourself in Court: How to Prepare & Try a Winning Case	$29.95	RYC
The Criminal Law Handbook: Know Your Rights, Survive the System	$24.95	KYR

HOMEOWNERS, LANDLORDS & TENANTS

	PRICE	CODE
The Deeds Book (California Edition)	$16.95	DEED
Dog Law	$14.95	DOG
Every Landlord's Legal Guide (National Edition)	$34.95	ELLI
Every Tenant's Legal Guide	$24.95	EVTEN
For Sale by Owner (California Edition)	$24.95	FSBO
Homestead Your House (California Edition)	$9.95	HOME
How to Buy a House in California	$24.95	BHCA
The Landlord's Law Book, Vol. 1: Rights & Responsibilities (California Edition)	$34.95	LBRT
The Landlord's Law Book, Vol. 2: Evictions (California Edition)	$34.95	LBEV
Leases & Rental Agreements (Quick & Legal Series)	$18.95	LEAR
Neighbor Law: Fences, Trees, Boundaries & Noise	$18.95	NEI
Safe Homes, Safe Neighborhoods: Stopping Crime Where You Live	$14.95	SAFE
Tenants' Rights (California Edition)	$19.95	CTEN
Stop Foreclosure Now in California	$29.95	CLOS

HUMOR

	PRICE	CODE
29 Reasons Not to Go to Law School	$9.95	29R
Poetic Justice	$9.95	PJ

⌑ Book with disk

● Book with CD-ROM

		PRICE	CODE

IMMIGRATION

	PRICE	CODE
How to Get a Green Card: Legal Ways to Stay in the U.S.A.	$24.95	GRN
U.S. Immigration Made Easy	$39.95	IMEZ

MONEY MATTERS

	PRICE	CODE
⌑ 101 Law Forms for Personal Use: Quick and Legal Series (Book with disk)	$24.95	101LAW
Chapter 13 Bankruptcy: Repay Your Debts	$29.95	CH13
Credit Repair (Quick & Legal Series)	$15.95	CREP
The Financial Power of Attorney Workbook	$24.95	FINPOA
How to File for Bankruptcy	$26.95	HFB
Money Troubles: Legal Strategies to Cope With Your Debts	$19.95	MT
Nolo's Law Form Kit: Personal Bankruptcy	$14.95	KBNK
Stand Up to the IRS	$24.95	SIRS

PATENTS AND COPYRIGHTS

	PRICE	CODE
The Copyright Handbook: How to Protect and Use Written Works	$29.95	COHA
Copyright Your Software	$39.95	CYS
⌑ License Your Invention (Book w/Disk)	$39.95	LICE
The Patent Drawing Book	$29.95	DRAW
Patent, Copyright & Trademark: A Desk Reference to Intellectual Property Law	$24.95	PCTM
Patent It Yourself	$44.95	PAT
⌑ Software Development: A Legal Guide (Book with disk—PC)	$44.95	SFT
The Inventor's Notebook	$19.95	INOT

RESEARCH & REFERENCE

	PRICE	CODE
● Government on the Net, (Book w/CD-ROM—Windows/Macintosh)	$39.95	GONE
● Law on the Net, (Book w/CD-ROM—Windows/Macintosh)	$39.95	LAWN
Legal Research: How to Find & Understand the Law	$19.95	LRES
Legal Research Made Easy (Video)	$89.95	LRME

SENIORS

	PRICE	CODE
Beat the Nursing Home Trap	$18.95	ELD
Social Security, Medicare & Pensions	$19.95	SOA
The Conservatorship Book (California Edition)	$29.95	CNSV

SOFTWARE
Call or check our website for special discounts on Software!

	PRICE	CODE
California Incorporator 2.0—DOS	$79.95	INCI
Living Trust Maker 2.0—Macintosh	$79.95	LTM2
Living Trust Maker 2.0—Windows	$79.95	LTWI2
Small Business Legal Pro Deluxe CD—Windows/Macintosh CD-ROM	$79.95	SBCD
Nolo's Partnership Maker 1.0—DOS	$79.95	PAGI1
Personal RecordKeeper 4.0—Macintosh	$49.95	RKM4
Personal RecordKeeper 4.0—Windows	$49.95	RKP4
Patent It Yourself 1.0—Windows	$229.95	PYP12
WillMaker 6.0	$69.95	WD6

Special Upgrade Offer
Get 25% off the latest edition of your Nolo book

It's important to have the most current legal information. Because laws and legal procedures change often, we update our books regularly. To help keep you up-to-date we are extending this special upgrade offer. Cut out and mail the title portion of the cover of your old Nolo book and we'll give you 25% off the retail price of the NEW EDITION of that book when you purchase directly from us. For more information call us at 1-800-992-6656. This offer is to individuals only.

⌑ Book with disk
● Book with CD-ROM

ORDER FORM

Code	Quantity	Title	Unit price	Total
		Subtotal		
		California residents add Sales Tax		
		Basic Shipping (*$6.00 for 1 item; $7.00 for 2 or more*)		
		UPS RUSH delivery $7.50–any size order*		
		TOTAL		

Name

Address

(UPS to street address, Priority Mail to P.O. boxes)   * Delivered in 3 business days from receipt of order. S.F. Bay Area use regular shipping.

FOR FASTER SERVICE, USE YOUR CREDIT CARD AND OUR TOLL-FREE NUMBERS

Order 24 hours a day	1-800-992-6656
Fax your order	1-800-645-0895
e-mail	cs@nolo.com
General Information	1-510-549-1976
Customer Service	1-800-728-3555, Mon.-Fri. 9am-5pm, PST

METHOD OF PAYMENT

☐ Check enclosed

☐ VISA   ☐ MasterCard   ☐ Discover Card   ☐ American Express

Account #   Expiration Date

Authorizing Signature

Daytime Phone

PRICES SUBJECT TO CHANGE.

VISIT OUR OUTLET STORES!   VISIT US ONLINE!

You'll find our complete line of books and software, all at a discount.

BERKELEY
950 Parker Street
Berkeley, CA 94710
1-510-704-2248

SAN JOSE
111 N. Market Street, #115
San Jose, CA 95113
1-408-271-7240

on the Internet
www.nolo.com

NOLO PRESS 950 PARKER ST., BERKELEY, CA 94710

Take a minute & Get a 1-year
Nolo *News* subscription free!*

With our quarterly magazine, the **NOLO** *News*, you'll

- **Learn** about important legal changes that affect you
- **Find out first** about new Nolo products
- **Keep current** with practical articles on everyday law
- **Get answers** to your legal questions in Ask Auntie Nolo's advice column
- **Save money** with special Subscriber Only discounts
- **Tickle your funny bone** with our famous Lawyer Joke column.

It only takes a minute to reserve your free 1-year subscription or to extend your **NOLO** *News* subscription.

CALL	FAX	E-MAIL	OR MAIL US THIS REGISTRATION CARD
1-800-992-6656	**1-800-645-0895**	**NOLOSUB@NOLOPRESS.com**	

 *U.S. ADDRESSES ONLY. ONE YEAR INTERNATIONAL SUBSCRIPTIONS: CANADA & MEXICO $10.00; ALL OTHER FOREIGN ADDRESSES $20.00.

fold here

- -

NOLO
PRESS

REGISTRATION CARD

NAME _____ DATE _____

ADDRESS _____

_____

CITY _____ STATE _____ ZIP _____

PHONE _____ E-MAIL _____

WHERE DID YOU HEAR ABOUT THIS PRODUCT? _____

WHERE DID YOU PURCHASE THIS PRODUCT? _____

DID YOU CONSULT A LAWYER? (PLEASE CIRCLE ONE)   YES   NO   NOT APPLICABLE

DID YOU FIND THIS BOOK HELPFUL?   (VERY)   5   4   3   2   1   (NOT AT ALL)

SUGGESTIONS FOR IMPROVING THIS PRODUCT _____

_____

WAS IT EASY TO USE?   (VERY EASY)   5   4   3   2   1   (VERY DIFFICULT)

DO YOU OWN A COMPUTER? IF SO, WHICH FORMAT? (PLEASE CIRCLE ONE)   WINDOWS   DOS   MAC

❑ We occasionally make our mailing list available to carefully selected companies. If you do not wish to receive mailings from these companies, please check this box.

❑ You can quote me in future Nolo Press promotional materials. Daytime phone number _____.   KWL

NOLO IN THE NEWS

"**N**olo helps lay people perform legal tasks without the aid—or fees—of lawyers."

—USA TODAY

Nolo books are ..."written in plain language, free of legal mumbo jumbo, and spiced with witty personal observations."

—ASSOCIATED PRESS

"...Nolo publications...guide people simply through the how, when, where and why of law."

—WASHINGTON POST

"Increasingly, people who are not lawyers are performing tasks usually regarded as legal work... And consumers, using books like Nolo's, do routine legal work themselves."

—NEW YORK TIMES

"...All of [Nolo's] books are easy-to-understand, are updated regularly, provide pull-out forms...and are often quite moving in their sense of compassion for the struggles of the lay reader."

—SAN FRANCISCO CHRONICLE

- - - - - - - - - - - - - - - fold here -

NOLO PRESS
950 Parker Street
Berkeley, CA 94710-9867

Attn: KWL